TO Gill,

OFF we go

TO THE STARS

W9-AWE-940

Hard
Market
Selling

Scott M. Primiano

Hard Market Selling

*Thriving in the
New Insurance Era*

Scott M. Primiano

Polestar Publications
Doylestown, Pennsylvania
2003

Copyright 2003 Scott Primiano. Printed and bound in the United States of America. All rights reserved. No part of this book may be reproduced or transmitted in any form or by any means, electronic or mechanical, including photocopying, recording, or by an information storage and retrieval system – with the exception of a reviewer who may quote brief passages in a review to be printed in a newspaper or magazine – without written permission from the publisher.

For information, contact Polestar Performance Programs, 1 - 800 - 795 - 3553 or www.gopolestar.com.

This book includes information from many sources and gathered from many personal experiences. It is published for general reference and is not intended to be a substitute for independent verification by readers when necessary and appropriate. The book is sold with the understanding that the neither the author nor publisher is engaged in rendering any legal, psychological, or accounting advice. The publisher and author disclaims any personal liability, directly or indirectly, for advice or information presented within. Although the author and publisher have prepared this manuscript with utmost care and diligence and have made every effort to ensure the accuracy and completeness of the information contained within, we assume no responsibility for error, inaccuracies, omissions, or inconsistencies.

ISBN: 0-9729555-0-X

ATTENTION: QUANTITY DISCOUNTS ARE AVAILABLE TO YOUR COMPANY OR EDUCATIONAL INSTITUTION for reselling, educational purposes, subscription incentives, gifts, or fund raising campaigns.
Please contact the publisher at Polestar Performance Programs, 1 - 800 - 795 - 3553 or www.gopolestar.com

Dedication

Although I conquer all the earth,
Yet for me there is only one city.
In that city there is for me only one house;
And in that house, one room only;
And in that room, a bed.
And one woman sleeps there,
The shining joy and jewel of all my kingdom.
— *Sanskrit Poem translated by John Brough*

For my magnificent MaryAnne. You are the wellspring of my inspiration, the fabric of my heart, and the magic in my soul. I am blessed by your grace and eternally grateful for your love.

Hard Market Selling

Table of Contents

Acknowledgements:

> *"Friendship is the allay of our sorrows, the ease*
> *of our passions, the discharge of our oppressions,*
> *the sanctuary to our calamities, the counselor of*
> *our doubts, the clarity of our minds, the emission*
> *of our thoughts, the exercise and improvement of*
> *what we dedicate".*
>
> – Jeremy Taylor

A very special thank you to my cherished friends for your collaboration and contributions to this book.

Brian O'Connell of Deadlines Ink, the finest freelance writer in the east, for bringing the words to life and for giving the book a personality. Your expertise as writer, editor, mentor, and "team-captain" are only surpassed by your sincerity, integrity, and friendship.

Angela Werner and Michael Hohne of Michael Hohne Design, for converting the manuscript into a perfectly designed book – cover to cover. Your creativity and technical ingenuity truly carried the book and the website to an unexpected level of professionalism and credibility. You are magnificent people with extraordinary talent and vision.

Patty, John, & Katie Harr – for your untiring effort and creative energy displayed at every stage of our development. We are honored and blessed to have you on our team.

MaryAnne DiCanto – the most devoted editor, advisor, and colleague that one could ever hope to find. You are the ultimate partner.

Judith F. Reynolds – my remarkable mother, from my first breath to her last, the greatest source of optimism and encouragement that I ever had.

John M. Reynolds – your inexhaustible devotion to our family, your influence as a writer, and your acceptance of me as your child and as your friend is an inspiration and a blessing.

Warren M. Primiano – for helping me to discover and embrace my destiny with grace and compassion and for teaching me to believe in my ability.

My Sons and Daughters – you are by far my greatest treasure and my constant source of pride and joy. It is you who nourish my soul and expand my heart.

Richard A. Coskren – friend, client, colleague and trusted advisor. Your support and encouragement is truly extraordinary and deeply appreciated.

Ken Ewell – a model of integrity, professional credibility, and generosity. I am eternally grateful for your friendship, guidance, and trust.

Fleet Insurance Services (formally Meeker-Sharkey) – Thanks to you Tom Sharkey Sr., Tom Sharkey Jr., Jim O'Conner, Brian Leddy, Terence Brown, Pete Gruenberg, John Moore, John Redmond, Bob Nitti and all the members of our first and best program. You, my oldest clients and dear friends, provided me with the opportunity to advance this program within our industry. This book would not be a book without the push that you gave me and the support that you have always provided.

Harleysville Insurance Group – The finest executive team that I have ever met. Thank you Lee Patkus, Doug Gaudet, Keith Fry, Dave Bond, Tim O'Malley, Jeff Dupleck, Dick Dowd, Bill Hoos, Dave Hofmann, Chris Gold, Sean Tief, Bonnie Rankin, Steve Horner, and Deb Crum. Because of your unwavering trust and dedication to our initiative, you have taken the definition of success to an entirely new level. I am proud to know you and honored to have worked with you.

Scott Addis – thank you for introducing me to the needs assessment and for providing me with the proving ground to use it. From you I have learned the true meaning of extraordinary client stewardship.

Jim Kosa – a true believer and a devoted friend. Your courage, your strength, and your faith have wonderfully enriched my life.

Gary Cameron – friend, brother, and untiring supporter of all things worth while. Whenever I reached, I always found your hand.

— *Scott Primiano*
April 2003

Introduction

"When you're through changing,
you're through."

— Bruce Barton

Like other monumental business trends, it was inevitable. The excesses created by what Alan Greenspan dubbed an "irrationally exuberant" stock market and the soft insurance market that so typified the 90s had to give way to more sensible, secure, and economically favorable business practices. As the dot-com frenzy turned into a dot-bomb disaster for private and institutional investors, portfolio income evaporated for many insurance companies and catalyzed an industry-wide examination of precariously high combined ratios. This, in turn, sparked a re-underwriting effort for many carriers seeking to bridge the gap between premium income and losses.

As the industry and the economy began to stabilize, as the "back-to-basics" cultural shift began to gather momentum, our world and our thinking was forever changed by the events of September 11, 2001. The insurance industry—tethered to the fortunes of our economy and culture—has changed with it. Americans have gone from craving Internet stock options and window tables at Spago's to craving comfort, warmth, and security. Unprecedented losses from the attacks, combined with already poor combined-ratios created by the soft market, catapulted our industry into a financial crisis overnight, creating an instantly hard market that has bewildered clients, agencies, and companies alike.

As the new economy continues to emerge from the rubble, re-insurers, carriers, and agencies, along with the five million people working in the insurance industry, are scrambling to define their place in the market. Some see opportunity and are enthusiastically re-inventing themselves to harvest it. Others, still hanging on to dated perspectives and obsolete business practices, see only trouble and are fighting to survive.

If you are a member of our insurance industry, however you got here and however you feel about being here, this book has been written to help you. It will help you make the most out of where you are now, identify where to go next, and build a plan to get there.

Before I go any further in explaining what the book is, let me explain what it is not. *Hard Market Selling: Thriving In the New Insurance Era* is not another "how to" book about the process of selling and servicing insurance. There are already too many books available that offer technical descriptions of various selling methods and service gimmicks, and none of them effectively weigh in with any remedies for the real-life, day-to-day struggles of the professionals for whom the books are intended. There are an equal number of inspiring and insightful books that provide reasonable evidence of a universal order, promote spirituality, and delve shrewdly into the metaphysical forces that govern pre- and post-life existence—yet they neglect to address the importance of making a living during this life.

Compared to such books, *Hard Market Selling* is a radical departure. How so? *Hard Market Selling* is a "hands-on" book that is designed to bring both topics (methods and motivation) together in the context of the down-to-earth reality experienced by the average producer, underwriter, account executive, agency principal, and customer service representative. It is an insider's guide for survival and achievement within an industry that is rapidly redefining itself.

The advantages of this book reach beyond the ranks of producers and service providers. Although the book has been written primarily for those directly involved with selling and servicing insurance programs, experience with our in-person training program (upon which the book is based) has proven that exposing the entire organization to these concepts has sparked some surprising results. Most non-service and non-sales people find the material quite easy to adapt to their situations and almost all of them undergo a positive transformation.

By and large, insurance producers, production underwriters, agency owners, and account executives stand to gain the most from this book. Why have I chosen to focus on these industry professionals? Frankly, I stand in awe of the really great ones, the *insurance fundamentalists* who go to work each day to make our world a safer place to live and to work. Unfortunately, not a lot of people recognize their contributions. It's the nature of the industry—do a great job of managing risk and … nothing happens. Buildings don't burn, employees don't slip and fall, trucks stay on the road, and so on. Our best work goes completely unnoticed.

This is particularly true of producers. People seem to forget that producers are people first. They are people with personal worth and integrity who are too often stereotyped as superficial and sordid, gluttonous and contemptible. Not so. Producers are people with families, car payments, and mortgages just like everybody else. Like career people everywhere, they are constantly being torn between the needs of their families and the needs of their clients and employers. They are people seeking acceptance, but who often meet rejection. They cannot be defined simply by their sales reports, and yet they are driven by their sales success. These are the people I work with everyday and the book is about what I have learned from them.

Now a little about me. For the past decade I have been employed as a performance coach, consultant, and speaker. What I have really been is a student of the people who sell and service—and the organizations for whom they sell and provide service. Thousands of hours spent in private sessions with insurance people at all levels combined with my own selling experience confirm the need for this book. It develops a long-term strategy for personal and professional success.

The book is laid out in a handy, real-world manner that makes the information inside these pages easy to understand and apply. Each section of the book presents a specific topic or concept that every insurance professional wrestles with at some level—either personally or professionally. The illustrations and anecdotes that describe how the issues translate into daily life are introduced by using examples with which they can identify and appreciate. They know these stories because they live them, and they know the pressures because they feel them.

Unfortunately, too many of them feel powerless to resolve these problems on their own. Years of working furiously in a soft market have left them out-of-balance and feeling disenfranchised from an industry that promised a career. The lingering effects of September 11, 2001, haven't helped either. We all lost somebody on that day—brothers and sisters in our industry— friends and colleagues that we may have never met but know nonetheless.

We know we have a job to do and we know it must be done in spite of political, social, and military events. We know the "right way" to conduct business, provide value, and build proper insurance programs; however, prevailing insurance buying and selling practices do not encourage a principled approach or allow time to truly build integrity-based relationships. For too many people in our industry, the path that leads to personal and professional success has become either too difficult to find or too confusing to follow. Hence the "call to action" messages that weave their way into each section of this book, intended to shake them up and get them moving toward a solution.

The premise of this program is that our station in life, both profession-ally and personally, is of our own making. Once we can accept responsibility for where we are in life and where we have been, regardless of environmental conditions or outside influence, then we will begin to realize that we already have the solutions to most of our difficulties and problems. They reside within us and are available to us at any time, providing that we take the time to listen. We already know our strengths, our weaknesses, and the answers to most of life's questions. Call it instinct, call it Providence, call it the voice of reason, I call it soul. The important thing is to learn how to call up this reserve of knowledge and strength when it is needed and to use it wisely.

Of all working people, insurance professionals are most in need of soul-searching guidance. They live lives of constant competition and disparaging evaluations. They are always on stage, always in motion, and at the mercy of critics and supporters alike. All too often, while attempting to balance competing priorities and keeping everyone else pleased, they lose sight of their own needs and fail to recognize the value of their own existence. They take shortcuts they otherwise would not, make personal sacrifices that they should not, and renounce their freedom of choice, not seeing that they still have choices.

If you work in our industry, this book is written for you—to enlighten you, to empower you, to inspire you, to help you rediscover who you are and what is important in your life. Life's questions all have answers and you should begin to find some of those answers here. Recent events notwith-standing, the world is basically a neutral place; we and we alone are respon-sible for who we are and what we become. That is my message and the focus of this book. I have been lucky enough to make a career out of these ideas, and I have done so joyfully and successfully. I share them with you now to remind you, to refresh you, and to challenge you to simply listen and take notice of where you are, why you are there, and where you are going.

Chapter One

Industry Observations: The Dawn of the New Insurance Era

*"The essence of all growth is the willingness
to make a change for the better, and then an
unremitting willingness to shoulder whatever
responsibility this entails."*

— Bill Wilson

Even prior to 2001, the worst year for the insurance industry in memory, the outlook was hardly rosy for insurers. The paramount issue is that over the last decade we in the insurance industry have been wrestling with a soft, price-driven market. The results of this prolonged price war have been nearly catastrophic for agencies and carriers, causing many to discard sound underwriting practices and principled marketing strategies in favor of buying a place in the market.

Taking full advantage of the price opportunity at nearly every renewal, clients have learned to ignore or minimize the importance of long-term risk management programs. They have downgraded their loss control strategies and instead have focused on short-term pricing decisions. This unfortunate trend forced the industry into an extremely price competitive position and caused some severe realignments of market share. For starters, carriers that were willing to live off investment returns worked with agents to undercut reasonable pricing models and buy-up business in many markets—perhaps believing that rate increases could be applied at time of renewal to make up for the shortfall in pricing. Wrong. Producers in these agencies were taught to sell aggressively and to make price rather than service the top priority. Forced to compete against this strategy, other carriers and agencies followed suit, creating a gigantic decline in premiums and commissions across the industry.

"For over a decade we have been wrestling with a soft, price-driven market."

Seeking to replace the lost capital, dramatic cutbacks in service and support personnel resulted in diminished, reactive client service strategies that only repaired relationships and never built them. The quantity of clients and their premium dollars became an industry priority rather than the quality of the business. Impersonal marketing strategies and specialty programs focused on large audiences, pitching price and product, hoping to attract the critical mass that could justify the effort. Producers, underwriters, and service personnel became stretched beyond acceptable limits trying to pursue every hint of an opportunity while still trying to manage an increasingly volatile book. An avalanche of paper, fruitless activity, and wasted proposals that are the unavoidable byproducts of this methodology is still suffocating all of them.

"This upside-down, soft-market scenario has compromised prudent agency and carrier management practices, and enabled the market to over-shop."

As the market continues to harden, premiums will continue to rise for all clients—regardless of claims experience. This market correction will, however, stabilize at a lower level for client companies that have lower loss ratios and are considered healthy and therefore better risks, and at much higher levels for companies with higher loss ratios that are riskier. In addition to industry classification differences, carrier pricing for risk will be heavily influenced by the frequency and severity of claims along with the functional presence of proactive client risk management and loss control programs. Frankly, marketing people have been tossed out of the boardroom and underwriting is now back in charge of pricing.

The "limbo" dance is over.

Who will navigate the choppy waters the industry is experiencing—and survive to tell the tale? Client companies with active risk control programs will justifiably fare better in the matter of premiums paid while those without such programs will certainly pay more. Client service is critical too. Agencies and carriers that have proactively serviced their accounts will continue to do so and retain their book. Agencies and carriers that bring nothing more to the table than product and price will not be as fortunate. Placing under-priced, poor-performing risks in an unforgiving market will be very difficult at best and very expensive.

The Soft Market

- Caused by aggressive growth strategies.
- Governed by marketing objectives rather than sound underwriting principles.
- Fueled by foolishness and ego.

How did our industry get so far removed from sound insurance practices and principles? Who exactly was it that decided a combined ratio of 120% + was acceptable and that an underwriting profit was an unreasonable expectation? The success of the 80s left most companies with huge reserves of capital that were invested in aggressive stock market plays and growth strategies. Essentially the plans were designed for market penetration that necessarily entailed creating a price advantage to attract new business. This strategy is often used in the travel industry to beef up short-term demand or market share and it works if it **remains short-term** and largely exclusive. In our industry, it was tried by too many for too long.

This upside-down, soft-market scenario compromised prudent agency and carrier management practices, enabled the market to over-shop rather than properly address risk management issues, and created unrealistic expectations of agencies and underwriters. In short, everybody in the industry has been desperately scrambling for enough new business to fill the revenue void created by shrinking premiums and reduced commissions that are the legacy of the soft market. Unfortunately, claims costs have not shown similar reductions nor have claims experiences been reduced by the same margins.

The problem caused by the immediate hardening of the market is not, as commonly believed, the rate increases. They are justified and overdue. The problem is how to reeducate clients that have grown accustomed to underpaying for their coverage and the many producers who have forgotten how to sell value, integrity, and trust. Our program—the program that you'll learn in this book—is designed to fix this problem.

Client Reactions

- Clients have come to expect slow or no service, renewal-based producer contact, and level or reduced pricing.
- Clients view their insurance program as a value-less commodity.
- Clients rely on market pressure rather than risk management and loss controls to contain insurance costs.

Presently, clients are reeling from the fallout of a market in transition. While they have certainly enjoyed the financial rewards of a buyers market, now that they are in a hard market, they consistently report feeling sold to and abandoned by producers that they trusted. That breach of trust compromises our most treasured asset—our personal integrity. As Peter Scotese, a retired Fortune 500 CEO once said, "Integrity is not a 90 percent thing, not a 95 percent thing; either you have it or you don't." Somewhere along the way, we seem to have lost it.

Consequently, buyer's remorse is high, service gaps are wide, and producers are collectively viewed as disingenuous. As a result, insurance buying practices have shifted away from consultative, relationship-centered, value-driven discussions and have moved toward commodity transactions that go to the lowest bidder. That, my friends, is a red flag of epic proportions for our industry.

So, what to do? Now that things are changing, insurance buying and selling practices must also be altered. We must all understand that client expectations regarding premium levels and "marketability" of their programs are universally in conflict with the new insurance economy.

Knowing this, we are obligated to explain the logic behind the pricing actions and to work with each client to develop effective risk management and loss control programs that will reduce loss ratios and contain insurance costs.

What Next?

- Carrier consolidation will continue, as will pricing actions.
- Carriers are re-underwriting books and consolidating service centers.
- Combined Ratios <u>must</u> continue to improve.

- Agencies and producers must step up proactive services to earn their keep.

In the soft market, many clients were willing to sacrifice value-driven service to get a reduced rate. They expected nothing more than the lowest price from their agent and their insurer. Now that the "lowest price" is at best an ambiguous term, all clients are going to expect agencies, insurers, and producers to justify their value and earn their keep. The question is … who is ready to deliver?

Additional Challenges

- Clients are facing "market correction" premium increases that appear "unjustified".
- All agencies will be squeezed toward a narrowing band of opportunity in the middle market.
- Personal lines, auto, and BOPs will continue to migrate to the internet.
- Lower middle market and small accounts will consolidate in carrier service centers and with banks that have entered the market.
- Large accounts will seek alternative markets and self-insurance programs.
- Reinsurers will begin to sell directly to the consumer market.
- Producers must do more than shop a policy; Clients and Carriers demand something more.
- Agencies must **stop selling insurance** and start reducing risk.

Complicating matters even further, the industry is currently experiencing dramatic changes in the distribution channels used to deliver products and service. Massive consolidations in small accounts and program business will continue to apply pressure at the low-end of the middle market. Large banks, carrier service centers, and internet insurance providers will soak up what is left of the small market and push onward toward the middle market, leaving no room for an inefficient legacy agency system. As might be expected, large accounts will turn to captives and alternative markets rather than stick with traditional insurance programs. We also see reinsurers dipping into the larger accounts at the top end of the middle market and actively courting some direct business.

Clearly then, the middle market is shrinking and inevitably this means that the number of agencies and producers competing successfully in this market must shrink as well. Who will prosper and who will fail? Years of observation and experiences in and around agencies of all sizes, specialties, and operating cultures give us a very clear picture of the type of agency that will be successful in the new insurance economy. This type of agency we call "healthy and thriving". As producer behavior tends to mirror agency attitudes, it is important that **everybody** learns to recognize and demonstrate the habits and behaviors that make for a healthy and thriving agency. When this is done correctly, everybody wins.

We also have a good understanding of those agencies that will struggle, perhaps fail, and why they will do so. We have labeled this a "legacy agency". Let's take a look at a legacy culture first.

The Legacy Agency:

- See the entire market as potential opportunity.
- Sporadic, traditional, volume-driven sales and marketing initiatives.
- Loosely networked and randomly referred.
- Targets new business during "hunting season".
- Policy, price, and product focused - Producers "hit-and-run".
- Service is reactive and often anonymous.
- Very limited client contact or involvement.
- Limited or no community or industry involvement.
- Unprofitable or marginally profitable book of business.
- Difficulty placing renewal business in a hard market.

Legacy agencies have reacted adversely to the soft market and are struggling to find some stability. They feel besieged by unrelenting competition, lack a strategic plan, and put most of their energy into chasing new business. They know that service is critical yet they lack the time and the personnel to provide anything other than reactive service that repairs, but never builds. They are rushed, exhausted, and worried. These agents sell rather than develop client relationships and they do so during the traditional selling season, 90-120 days prior to renewal.

There are no proactive risk management or loss control programs for their clients nor are they able to consistently deliver value-added services.

Their book of business is inconsistent in regard to business mix or specialty, tends to run an above average loss ratio, and, in this market, is difficult to place at time of renewal. They focus on price and volume. Some of them are established agencies trying to replace the flow of departing clients and others are newer agencies trying to grow in an unforgiving market. They are desperately looking for some relief and many honestly wish to conduct themselves like the top performers; they simply don't know how. Others can't or won't.

Now let's look at a healthy and thriving agency:

The Healthy Agency:

- Highly selective when choosing opportunities.
- Little or no marketing.
- Heavy use of network and referrals.
- Conducts formal and comprehensive needs analysis.
- Does not "sell" insurance, offers risk management services.
- Active on Client committees and boards.
- Active in community and industry.
- Developes proactive client service plans for all clients.
- No time-line on sales process.
- Low volume, carefully coordinated.
- Manages a profitable, carefully selected book of business.
- Partners with carriers at renewal time.

A healthy book of business is not discovered—it is developed. It is also characteristic of a healthy agency. Successful agents have been able to avoid the feeding frenzy created by the soft market and the financial hardship that accompanies it by investing their time and energy into the client organizations that created their success.

They save their clients money through sound risk management practices rather than shifting markets and they have established a service reputation that is beyond reproach. New business opportunities flow to these agents through a referral network and they are discriminating when selecting which opportunities to pursue. They tend to avoid the bidding process, as do their clients, choosing instead to build steadfast relationships that extend beyond insurance.

As the market firms, these agencies continue to thrive as the integrity of their risk management and loss control programs greatly enhance risk evaluation, book profitability, and carrier relationships. They are proactive, efficient, creative, and energetic. These agencies are financially sound, expertly managed, and culturally nourishing for clients, carriers, and employees.

A Vision For You:

The following is a summary review of the client discovery, development, and management strategies used by top producers working in healthy and thriving agencies. Although I have broken down the process into four distinct stages, it is important to note that the sales and service behaviors demonstrated during each stage of the model are on a continuum, overlapping and blending with each other throughout the process. This is the model that we will follow when building your marketing, sales, and service programs.

Program Overview:

Success, as we define it, means consistent and efficient growth in new business, profit, and client retention over time. Therefore, the marketing, selling, and service activities that create and maintain the desired growth must also be consistent, efficient, and lasting.

Top producers know that a random and haphazard approach to marketing leads to random and haphazard results. They recognize that consistency is created when marketing, sales, and service plans are aligned, interwoven, and constructed to ensure that each client contact builds from the last and leads to the next. They see that traditional selling practices that identify a prospect, lead the prospect to a sale, and then drop the new client in the lap of an unknown service team while the producer moves on to the next prospect, violates the integrity of the relationship and destroys producer credibility. Top producers understand that real opportunity is developed long after the initial sales event because consistent, proactive, personalized, value-driven, client contact beyond the first sale continues to build client trust and naturally develop into cross-selling, referral, and networking opportunities while ensuring a stellar retention rate.

Top producers know that their success is only a byproduct of their clients' success and of the win/win relationship that they create and maintain. The service plan of a top producer is almost identical to the sales plan. The activities use to create the relationship are the same ones used to maintain it because that is what attracted the client and will retain the client. When the client handed over the broker-of-record letter, he was not buying insurance—he was buying into the relationship with the producer based upon a demonstrated level of value that met or exceeded expectations.

At a minimum, the client expects more of the same. Top producers know this and devote their time exclusively to activities that proactively build and maintain client relationships. The following is a glimpse of what "business as usual" will mean for you, a top-producer, at each stage of the process:

Stage One – Marketing and Prospecting

Effectively communicating a distinctive message to potential clients is, by far, the greatest challenge that a producer is forced to contend with. Clients are the constant targets of insurance salespeople and their intrusive and impersonal mass-marketing weapons, such as the cold call and the mail blitz.

Recognizing that the problem with most sales and service plans is that they are the products of these inept, inefficient, and inconsistent marketing strategies that are labor intensive and create a mostly wasted exposure and fruitless follow-up, you will opt for a more refined approach.

Your creative, functional, and effective marketing plans begin with a narrow definition of who your clients are going to be. You research your target market in advance and limit your marketing resources to a discrete handful of pre-qualified prospects, specifically selecting your clients rather than waiting to be selected by a client of unknown quality who is responding to a generalized marketing message. This enables you to build a highly personalized, disciplined, and manageable marketing strategy. You use a scalpel where others use a machete.

Your pre-scheduled, carefully coordinated marketing events build on each other and occur in consistent waves over time rather than in random mass blasts. Each of your contacts will be directly linked with a follow-up plan that is equally precise and easily managed due to the limited volume of prospective clients.

Rather than being aggressive, intrusive, and overwhelming, your approach is gentle and gradual, designed to attract the right clients to you for the right reasons over time. Your marketing initiatives are not intended to sell but instead to inform and educate your selected pool of prospects so that they have enough information to make an educated decision about your capabilities.

Your message is one of integrity, value, and trust. It is not about product, price, gimmicks, gloss, or glitter. You are establishing a rapport with dignity and professionalism—traits that will characterize your behavior and your relationships and allow you to rise above the noise of the marketplace.

Stage Two – Relationship Development

These are our moments of truth. What we do here and what we say here will determine if we stay in the relationship or if we are asked to leave. If we have done a thorough job of pre-screening for desirable clients, we already have a good idea that our client is qualified and worthy of our time and attention. Now we must prove ourselves worthy of theirs.

Conventional wisdom would have you selling from the moment that you enter the client's facility. Make nice with the receptionist, stand rather that sit in the waiting area, scan the office for hints of a personal life that you can make into small talk. You know this game and they know this game. Because the game is as trite as it sounds, you don't play.

Instead, you are going to start developing your relationship by demonstrating the unexpected levels of value and integrity that you intend to use to maintain it. You know that there is a long way to go before you are ready to make any qualified insurance program recommendations so you remove the sales event from your mind and focus on the client and their expectations.

Rather than wine them, dine them, and pitch them, you are going to listen to them. Using an agenda that outlines your process, you request permission to conduct a thorough needs analysis that includes a tour of the facility, employee interviews, risk management and loss control program assessments, claims analysis, and policy reviews. You will review your service plan, the client's expectations, and your ability to measure up to them. You will provide references without being asked, invite them to tour your agency, and introduce them to your service team. You will talk about the markets and let them meet with the underwriting team, loss control reps, and claims personnel. You can, of course, entertain them as well; however, your definition of entertainment reaches beyond the golf course or the ballpark—it includes loss control seminars, client roundtables, and attendance at their safety committee meetings.

Having concluded your assessment, you know your client's corporate philosophy, structure, and exposures. You have the information that you need to look beyond the issues of policies and rates because you have gained a true understanding of your client's organizational culture and specific needs. This insight will enable you to specifically tailor programs and strategies that meet or exceed your client's expectations. Now it is okay to talk about insurance.

Stage Three – Value-Added Service Delivery

It is at this stage that the breech of trust between the client and the producer usually occurs. The check is banked, the binder is in, and the policy and endorsements are on the way. The producer is feeling good, anticipating the commission, and ready to move along to the next prospect looking for more of the same. The account is assigned to a CSR and off they go, whistling while they work, sorting through the next batch of targets.

But ... what about the new client? How are they feeling now that the deal is sealed? Regardless of the job that was done to build the relationship and put together the program, despite the smiles, handshakes, and pats-on-the-back that were exchanged once the account sold, something mysterious is happening back at the client's office. Something that most producers don't learn about until it's too late.

Buyer's remorse. A sinking post-purchase feeling that casts doubt on the deal and raises suspicions about your character. It is a factor in every transaction and it could significantly damage the relationship if it is left unabated.

You, of course, know this and have the time to do something about it. You know that it takes much more than a "thank you card" to clear this hurdle. You know that it takes an immediate and unsolicited demonstration of value that will evidence your commitment and help the client to remember why you have been selected as the broker-of-record. And this is just the beginning. From this moment on you will be proactively visible and viable. You will sit on the safety committee, conduct claims reviews, write a disaster plan, develop a substance abuse policy, conduct employment practices audits, ensure that your client is OSHA compliant, and install a driver safety program. You won't do all the work, of course, but you will see that it is done.

Your client will finally feel in control of insurance costs and experience a tremendous sense of satisfaction from knowing that somebody else (you and your team) is thinking about their insurance program, every hour of every day. And you will be rewarded with referrals and introductions to others that need the same level of integrity, value, and trust. Your work will uncover additional insurance needs and you will effortlessly cross-sell. Your status will be elevated from insurance salesperson to trusted advisor and you will be immune to competition. You will also be quite unique. Only the best producers ever take the time to fully develop client relationships to this level. They know that their relationships are most vulnerable immediately after the initial sale and they know that renewals are won and lost early on, not in the 60-90 days before the expiration date that most producers use as a guide. They know, and now you know.

Stage Four – Relationship Maintenance

Your relationship with your client is now on solid ground. As the hunting season draws near and competitors start making their rounds, your team is busy comparing your performance to the benchmarks that were established early in the relationship. You are also developing new program guidelines and designing enhanced coverage for the coming year. Your renewal meeting with the client will not be the worrisome event that it is for many producers because you have proven worthy and effective. For you, it is just another day.

Your value-added service programs are in full gear and you are preparing for your renewal strategy session. Taking nothing for granted, you revisit some of the steps encountered during the initial proposal process and design an enhanced value-added service schedule for the coming year. You conduct a final claims review and analyze the reserves. You meet with the carrier and the client together to review the policies and establish new risk management and loss control objectives for the coming year. You do all of this because it is the right thing to do and it is a natural extension of your value commitment to the client, not because you are afraid of losing the account.

As you review the year, you analyze your own performance and your personal objectives. This critique clearly shows what worked, what didn't work, and how you can evolve your plans to find even greater productivity, efficiency, and success.

You see how the relationships with your clients blossomed under ever-increasing levels of value, integrity, and trust. You see how careful client selection from the very start enabled you to devote the time required to manage your relationships proactively and consistently. You see how a comprehensive approach to developing your proposals enabled you to learn and understand your clients' operations, industry, culture, policies, procedures, and risk management goals prior to developing your recommendations. Your awareness of your clients' needs and expectations allowed you to build a customized strategy to meet and exceed them. Clearly, you have broken through the crowd and discovered not just a new way, but the right way to create and maintain desirable client relationships.

...And Away We Go

The *Hard Market Selling* model was developed to improve the way that insurance is bought and sold by injecting into the process an ever-increasing level of value, integrity, and trust. Experience has shown that agencies and carriers that proactively seek, sell, and service clients by consistently demonstrating high levels of value, integrity, and trust attract and retain desirable business. Unfortunately, this message has often been overshadowed by a widespread industry practice that myopically focuses on getting any and all business on the books as soon as possible without regard for any long-term impact on agency or carrier prosperity.

If you then factor in the effects of the current market changes that require ever increasing levels of account profitability and agent and client accountability, you begin to see an industry shakeout where uninformed and unengaged agencies and carriers will pay a serious price in lost profitability. The pendulum has swung back to sound insurance principles that require all of us to manage the cost of insurance by managing the frequency and severity of claims. We can forecast stormy weather for agencies and carriers that are unwilling or unable to adopt a disciplined, proactive, consistently value-added service strategy for their clients.

And now it is time to begin ...

Chapter Two

How To Use This Book

"Start by doing what's necessary, then what's possible, and suddenly you are doing the impossible."

— St Francis of Assisi

Because positions, responsibilities, and needs vary significantly between commercial lines producers, production underwriters, benefits consultants, personal lines producers, customer service representatives, account executives, carrier marketing managers, agency principals, and so on, one book cannot address the specifics of each position or for every line of business in our industry.

With this in mind, I have written *Hard Market Selling* from the perspective of a typical commercial lines producer. Believing their world to be as close to the middle of the road as one will find, and knowing it to be the most volatile at the present time, I believe that the need for this new approach is most obvious for all readers when presented in this context.

Now what about you? How do you apply the suggestions, strategies, and activities to your specific set of circumstances? Because we work with carriers, agencies, underwriters, and sales and service professionals from every segment of our industry, we are able to provide each participant in our in-person training and consulting programs with some techniques for personalizing the program. I'm going to do the same for you here to help you squeeze as much value out of the material as you possibly can. The following are your guidelines for personalizing your own program:

Rule #1:

You are unique. So is your perspective, environment, experience, personality, preference, lifestyle, and so on. Rather than adjust who you are to conform with my recommendations, I'd like you to adjust my recommendations to fit who you are and the circumstances that you face each day. It is not my intention to lock you into a prescribed process that might be inappropriate or inadequate for your needs. I have defined our objective; our ultimate destination, however, there are an infinite number of roads to take to get there. You are the navigator. I have presented you with a buffet of ideas and a range of strategies. Select those that you need and can apply, adapt them to fit your world, and move forward according to your plan.

Rule #2:

There is something here for everybody. Your work is only what you do, it is not who you are. The personal growth and development content is the heart of this book and I believe it to be the most valuable. The personal objectives that you are coached to identify define you and the meaning of your life. Your satisfaction and happiness depend on your ability to accomplish these goals and I want you to be successful. The goal setting, planning, and priority management tools have been designed to help *you the person* first, and *you the professional* second.

Guidelines for Underwriting Professionals:

For you, the hard market has led to an avalanche of submissions, massive re-underwriting, strict appetite guidelines, and a disrupted agency plant. Ouch. Painful, but necessary. Many of you are pinned down by the volume of the processing that needs to get done and you are scrambling to provide baseline levels of service to your agents and insureds. Endorsement processing is lagging, renewals are extraordinarily time consuming and often late, new business opportunities are piling up, the phone doesn't stop ringing, and no matter how hard you work, there doesn't appear to be an end in sight. Real issues that require real solutions.

An unnecessary but common response to this workflow crisis has been to focus on the processing. Field underwriting and agency plant management activities have taken a back seat to desk underwriting and processing files. Unfortunately, effective and strategic communication between agencies and carriers is abysmal at a time when it should be a priority.

There is a solution and it can be found in the pages of this book. When reading the material, I suggest that you think of it in terms of carrier-to-agent relationships rather than in the agent-to-insured context that is presented. The parallels are quite apparent and the strategies are easy to develop when viewed from this perspective.

For example, agents will be building a value-added service plan for their key accounts. You will be building an agency management plan for your key agency relationships. I suggest in no uncertain terms that agents must protect their time (their most valuable resource) by allocating it only to those clients that are worthy of it. The same holds true for you.

You must make a determined effort to segment your agency plant and evaluate which agency relationships truly qualify as partnerships and then prioritize your investment of time and attention to these agencies. As we shake off the legacy of the soft market and confront the operational challenges created by the hard market, recognize that legacy behaviors, assumptions, and procedures are no longer appropriate for this new insurance era. The first thing to go must be the erroneous assumption that you the carrier are able to provide and should try to provide the same level of services, proactive or otherwise, to every agency that hangs up your plaque. You simply don't have time nor are you compensated enough for your effort. Agents pay for your time and they pay for it with premium dollars from new and existing business. Spending time with those that attract and retain desirable business means less time spent with those who don't. Otherwise, you end up over-servicing half of your plant and under-servicing the other half.

Here are some more ideas to consider when implementing this material:

> Prioritize your new business submissions based upon the opportunity and the agent rather than the old "first in first out" rule of thumb. Your best agents bring you your real opportunities and these should not be squandered while you work on submissions from other agents that don't fit your appetite, are incomplete, wishful thinking, or intended only to be sold off of rather than sold. Triage your new business submissions, get rid of the junk quickly, and focus on taking care of those that will take care of you. The opportunity cost for not doing so is horrific and the real goal is not to process paper, it is to write qualified, profitable new business.

You don't have time to chase. Too much time is wasted reminding agents over and over again that you have submission standards that mandate specific information to be included in all submissions. Most of the required information is commonly requested by all carriers and should be obvious. Agents that consistently fail to comply and require chronic follow-up to "remind" them of what you are missing are wasting your time. Particularly if they don't sell the account, which is too often the case. The days of the "courtesy quote" and the "quote pending" need to end. You are better than that and so are they. Let the incomplete stuff sit while you work on the real opportunity. If the agent is serious about writing the account, they will get you what you need.

Get back to the field. Too many of you are caught behind your desk trying in vain to stay in contact with your agency plant. It's not working. Your agencies need consistent coaching, training, and support if they are going to represent you effectively and with integrity. You must assume an active role in helping them manage their book of business through these uncertain times. Carriers need to maximize their visibility and viability with their key agents by proactively supplying them with the loss control and risk management resources that they need to do the job the way that I suggest that it be done. CSRs need further training on submission standards, coverage changes, and appetite guidelines. Pre-renewal strategy sessions, joint calls for new business and renewal presentations, joint business plan reviews, and agency performance evaluations are all essential elements of a true partnership, none of which can be done by exchanging voice-mail. Again, this means less or no time spent with those that are not productive, even if they are demanding more of it. Some of your lower tier, non-productive agents can rise to the occasion and become valued partners. Some will be worthy of your effort to rehab them, but most won't, so pick your spots very carefully and hold them accountable for improving their results.

Use the material presented in the book to formulate your agency management plans. Develop a list of activities that will bring value to your key agency relationships by improving production, retention, profitability, and efficiency, and review these ideas with your agents. Following the format outlined in the book, conduct your needs assessment and develop these customized plans agency by agency.

Calendar the activities, execute, and monitor the results. Carriers that I am working with and have helped to develop this strategy are currently outperforming their expectations and their competitors, financially and culturally. Use the ideas contained in the channel marketing section to create your agency marketing plans and to help your key agents create their value-added marketing strategy for their clients. Build a needs assessment for them to use or, better yet, for your joint use on a co-developed opportunity. Use the referral harvesting strategy to develop a new agency appointment plan that keeps a steady flow of quality new agency prospects at your fingertips. These are new agencies that have been recommended by your best agents. Use the priority management system to organize yourself and your underwriting team and use the goal setting system to make sense of it all. I assure you, adopt this method of conducting business and conducting yourself and you will be well on your way to a more balanced, enjoyable, and successful personal and professional life.

Guidelines for Personal Lines Professionals:

Every strategy presented in the book can be directly applied to personal lines. However, the large number of clients that make up a standard book of personal lines business will prevent you from implementing an elaborately personalized plan for your clients. Instead, gear you efforts toward automated contact using email and the telephone. You can provide a tremendous amount of value by regularly mailing risk management information, surveys, and industry updates, and you can conduct educational seminars for your clients at regularly scheduled times during the year. The objective is to maintain consistent contact over time with your clients. The contact does not have to be complicated or inefficient.

Do plan on conducting a needs assessment and do build a value-added service plan; however, do not try to customize it for each client as we suggest for commercial lines producers. Keep it simple, efficient, and effective.

Guidelines for Employee Benefits Professionals:

Because almost every provider of employee benefits has a wide open distribution network as well as a direct sales team, differentiating on price, product, or anything other than value-added service is out of the question. Because of these unique characteristics of your sale, it will be difficult to claim a "specialty" in any particular space in the market that isn't already well populated with competitors. Therefore, complete implementation of each strategy presented in the book is vital for your success. Additionally, because the "end users" of your products are large employee populations rather than a small group of managers, your value-added service plans will be dominated by activities that educate and inform the entire client company. For you, being consistently visible and viable with the employee group will involve regularly scheduled employee meetings, brown-bag training sessions in their facility, focus groups and other satisfaction surveys, help with new enrollments, COBRA assistance, and so on. Your clients need a consultant much more than they need a salesperson, so … consult.

Guidelines for service and administrative professionals:

The traditional distinction between sales-related activities and service-related activities is removed in this model. The reasons for doing so are clearly defined in the material so I will not elaborate here other than to say that the old practice of a service person or service team coming into the client relationship to clean up after the producer when the deal is done are over. Your role in this model is as vital before the sale as it is after the sale and your ability to create and implement a value-added service plan is as important as any work that a producer will do. Please do not be thrown off by the title or the references to selling behavior; the material is appropriate for anybody, working anywhere, who is responsible for taking care of clients. I believe that you will find the program to be especially refreshing and validating.

It is not my intention for you to implement the systems and strategies exactly as I've presented them, nor are you expected to embrace all of these ideas at once. To do so would only add to your burden and, I believe, be self-defeating. Instead, ease your way into each new approach, one at a time, by adapting the material to fit who you are and the circumstances that you find yourself in. Take your time, be patient with yourself, and let your plans and strategies evolve.

> *"A complex system that works is invariably found*
> *to have evolved from a simple system that works."*
> — John Gall

Chapter Three

Managing Your Objectives

"Those who cannot tell what they desire or expect, still sigh and struggle with indefinite thoughts and vast wishes."
— Ralph Waldo Emerson

Remember that old quote from Thomas Edison—the one where he explained the concept of genius as "one percent inspiration and 99 percent perspiration"? I love that quote. What Edison is saying is that you have to work hard to achieve your goals—and so-called "geniuses" aren't exempt from applying a little elbow grease, too.

I'm reminded of the Edison quote because my objectives usually frighten people. Not because my objectives are sinister—they're not—rather it is their magnitude that can shake people up. Aiming high and hitting the mark isn't easy and often doesn't seem worth the effort. That said, I have never been one to settle for less, nor am I content with mediocre results. I believe, and my experience has proven, that all well-conceived goals are attainable, regardless of size—but you've got to work hard to attain them. All goals, big, small, and other, represent nothing more than a series of lesser objectives linked together to form a larger one. The larger the goal, the longer the chain.

Look at Apple Computers founder Steven Jobs. He was all of 12 years old when he called Bill Hewlett, founder of Hewlett-Packard, and asked if he could spare some new parts for a computer project Jobs was working on. That "project" was the personal computer. Even at a young age, Jobs knew that success is developed (not discovered) by starting early and working each link in the chain (or each step in the plan) consistently and thoroughly before moving onto the next.

A part here, some funding there, some advice over there—soon Jobs was on his way to building the first commercial personal computer and making history in the process.

Here's another, more personal example. My quest for a pilot's license began with finding a flight school, which encouraged me to find the money for tuition, which motivated me to allocate the time for study, which aided me in practicing the lessons, which developed my expertise, which in turn allowed me to pass the test that made me a licensed pilot—all according to plan. Well, almost according to plan. Actually, what began as a six-month plan turned into a three-year quest. As circumstances in my life changed (i.e. two relocations and a business start-up), so too did my plan have to be corrected to accommodate them.

> *"In this life we get only those things for which we hunt, for which we strive, and for which we are willing to sacrifice. It is better to aim for something that you want—even though you miss it—than to get something that you didn't aim to get, and which you don't want! If we look long enough for what we want in life we are almost sure to find it, no matter what that objective may be."*
> — George Mathew Adams

So it goes for most of our goals, particularly the large and long-term ones. Perfect execution according to plan is a nasty delusion—a monster myth that sets up lofty expectations that are bound to be disappointed. Disappointment leads to defeat—if you let it. There's an old story about the fabled 19th century British explorer Henry Morton Stanley, who after fighting his way through a deep and dangerous jungle, was asked if he'd been frightened and felt like giving up. "I don't think about it that way," he replied. "I did not raise my head to see the whole. I saw only this poisonous snake in front of me that I had to kill to take the next step. Only after I had gotten through did I look back and see what I had been through. Had I taken a look at the whole thing beforehand, I would have been so scared that I never would have attempted it."

Okay, there aren't any snakes in the insurance profession—not that crawl on their bellies, anyway. But that doesn't mean you should forego a plan—just be prepared to create a flexible one you can change on the fly. "If you ever want to make God laugh, tell him your plans" my friend Gary often says when the topic comes up. "Successful outcomes," he adds, "usually result from contingency planning and corrections to the original plan.

Demanding strict adherence to your original idea and expecting perfect compliance with your initial assumptions is a guarantee of disappointment and frustration." Things change. Conditions change. You have to be ready to change too.

But change what—and when? After an idea bubbles to the surface, it's difficult to say which goals will be easy and which will have you reaching for the aspirin. Proper timing has as much to do with success as any other factor, and careful planning of each step in the process, although not always accurate, is still mandatory.

> *"Difficulties mastered are opportunites won."*
> —Winston Churchill

Patience is crucial. My need for instant gratification has derailed projects that would have benefited from my having had an even-tempered disposition, and not the impatience of a child awaiting his sixth birthday party. I also know that an occasional lapse of self-discipline will cause me to become distracted by other activities. Such diversions serve only to take my eyes off the prize long enough to damage a project's timeline and its success.

Regardless of the cause, the effect of living with an unrealized goal is unbearable. It is unbearable because a legitimate goal never goes away until it is achieved. Left undone, it lives on as a regret. It invokes feelings of failure and resentment as we think about "what if?" and fantasize about "if only".

Over the years I've learned that one of the keys to success is not to become too rigid or too righteous about doing it "your way". Know at the beginning of any plan that unforeseen events and uncontrollable circumstances will occur and require you to change tactics and alter your plan. That's okay. Change is good. As George Bernard Shaw once said, "Progress is impossible without change and those that cannot change their minds cannot change anything." Change is difficult—as is achieving your goals. Almost every other major goal that I have set for myself has usually been difficult to achieve and, at times, seemed altogether impossible. Yet without goals we have no direction, no destination, no sense of purpose, and no hope of making the most out of life.

> *"What an immense power over a life is the power of*
> *possessing distinct aims. The voice, the dress, the*
> *look, the very motions of a person define and alter*
> *when he or she begins to live for a reason."*
> — Elizabeth Stuart Phelps

Back to Business

Think about it. Think about the history of selling and try to identify success stories that didn't involve goal setting. Actually, try to identify any success in life that didn't involve goal setting. Think about John Goddard. As a 15-year-old boy, the famous explorer established 127 "goals" he wanted to accomplish in life. They included navigating the Nile River, climbing Mount Everest, reading the bible, playing the piano, among others. At 75 years old, about the only thing he hadn't accomplished was visiting the moon. Goddard understood the importance of matching vision with purpose and calculated action. So too, have many of you in the sales world. It's no secret that sales professionals are routinely exposed to various goal setting systems, strategies, and techniques. Unfortunately, although logical in approach and principle, they all too often never grab hold long enough to become habit forming.

Why did the intrepid Goddard succeed when so many struggle with failure? The same reason why our New Year's resolutions, made with such sincerity, dissolve by Super Bowl Sunday and the same reason business plans, marketing programs, service contracts, and sales projections, are converted into filing cabinet fodder with such regularity.

Let me explain. Most goal setting systems that break down, either partially or completely, do so very predictably. As salespeople, our tendency is to focus on activities that generate an instant return for our time and attention. Whether real or perceived, the anticipation of our return, usually in the form of commission dollars or recognition, motivates us to devote our energy to short-term selling events. We equate today's success with tomorrow's check and learn early that more prospecting activity means more checks. Calling on a new prospect might pay quicker returns than further developing a current client. This is not perceived as a problem until the inevitable occurs—we begin to see clients slip away and our book of business beginning to erode.

As is the case with our personal relationships, our relationships with our clients thrive on our consideration or turn elsewhere for attention. Clients have demands for service, meetings, problem resolution, socializing, coaching, planning, training, and other contacts.

To provide this service, our focus must shift. If client retention is an objective, then we are forced to invest more time in relationship maintenance. The time we once used for pure sales production is now shared or even dominated by these service requirements. Adding to the burden, we have internal administrative requirements and external demands on our personal time. It seems that the more successful we become, the more difficult it is to remain a success.

> *"The barriers are not erected which can say to aspiring talents and industry, 'thus far and no further'."*
> — Ludwig Van Beethoven

How do sales professionals cope in such a chaotic environment? With uncertainty—and with mixed results. As new business production levels off or decreases, we struggle to find enough time to recommit to these business-building—and revenue-generating—activities. Now our sense of work ethic comes into play, though often that's hardly the issue. Knowing that more activity means greater success, we extend our days, and burn the proverbial midnight oil. We also add or request additional support, and begin to take shortcuts or put off administrative work, hoping against hope that all bases are covered and all potential cracks are sealed. At this point a mild sense of panic sets in. Panic is not good for anybody, especially a salesperson. As the unlucky-at-love 20-something career women puts it in the movie *Singles*, "desperation is the world's worst anti-perspirant".

Our desperation sets in when we realize that the bases aren't covered and the seals have cracks in them that are widening by the hour. We're in full reactive mode now, and we begin looking for a solution—any solution—that will turn us into the finely-tuned, humming-like-a-Swiss-watch production machine that we've been before. That quest for an alternative solution often ends at a goal-setting workshop, a time management seminar, or with the purchase of a quick fix, *Who Cheesed my Move?*-type book. We read, we listen, we absorb as best we can. Then we ring the bells and blow the whistles right on cue, and we wait for things to change. They don't. Our enthusiasm for the "new and improved" approach wanes with time until we find ourselves unceremoniously dumped right back to where it all began—at our own desks.

Harsh? Maybe so. But not uncommon. Not long ago, I went in search of a solution to this problem. This "cycle from Hell" had played out once too often in my own life, with feeble results. But what to do, I wondered? Simple. Declare war on every know-it-all-with-an-answer that ever sold a book or gave a speech. It was time to try something original.

> *"Sometimes if you want to see a change for the better,*
> *you have to take things into your own hands."*
> — Clint Eastwood

I began with a look at my personal goals and found nothing peculiar, puzzling, or inappropriate. Maybe my goals were a tad optimistic, (i.e. XX dollars in savings by age 45). Still, they were balanced against others that were simple and less daunting, like learning to juggle (rubber balls—not chainsaws). They were also equally divided between long-term objectives (run a complete marathon), and short-term ones, (visit Gettysburg). Some were one-timers (finish this book), while others were repetitive (work out four times per week). Some were very specific and measurable (my business plan), while others were less clearly defined (happy and healthy children). Finally, some were spiritual (meditate daily) while others were materialistic (a house at the beach).

A closer look revealed something interesting. In addition to being achievable and meaningful, each goal was in some way connected to the other (except for the juggling). My goal to run a marathon was consistent with working out four times a week, which meant that I had to quit smoking. Also, I had to eat a healthy diet to stay fit and to do the work that matched the plan that made the money to fund the trips and buy the stuff I wanted.

Now things were beginning to make sense. Each objective, large and small, personal or professional, supported the others. To successfully accomplish the large and long-term goals, I had to first accomplish the less imposing short-term goals, and maintain them consistently. I had to be a nurturer (who knew?). Happy and healthy children for instance, require happy and healthy parents who consistently allocate the time necessary to care for them. Same thing with my goals and me.

Let's take the parenting analogy a step further. The short-term objective is to regularly spend time with my children; the long-term goal, of course, is to provide them with a great start in life while helping them to avoid therapy, early wedlock, and jail time. Coming to see these connections was a meaningful awakening that led immediately to other discoveries.

By applying the parenting angle to my own situation, I realized that my professional objectives could not stand on their own merits. Instead, they needed to directly support my personal goals. I thought of the few positions I have held that required conforming my personal agenda to fit the demands of the job. Although each job seemed attractive and desirable when I started, none of them had ever worked out as planned, and all of them eventually proved unsatisfactory. Now I knew why.

My always-wiser-than-I-give-her-credit-for wife had cautioned me against confusing "who" I am with "what" I did for a living; faithfully reminding me that work was only a means to an end—something I did to facilitate the achievement of these life-defining objectives. Her voice echoed again the familiar nag ... did I say nag?—I mean mantra:

"Your legacy is your life's work, not your profession," she said, with only the slightest bit of exasperation "You will not be remembered for how well you did at work but for how well you did at life. Focus on life."

Okay, it took a while but this time I finally recognized the significance of these simple words. Let me write it down now before I have to be reminded again.

Whatever we put ahead of our personal objectives will ultimately stand in the way of their accomplishment. Work is indeed important, but only to the degree that it is effectively contributing to our larger need for personal satisfaction. If you make your job a higher priority than your family, you will lose a meaningful relationship with your family. When work is more important than your health, you get sick. When the Red Sox are more important than your sanity—well ... you get the picture. I realized that time away from work should be devoted to our personal agendas—not viewed as an opportunity to slip in even more work.

> *"The world basically and fundamentally is*
> *constituted on the basis of harmony. Everything*
> *works in co-operation with something else."*
> — Preston Bradley

I know what you're thinking. "He's off on some 'Zen and the Art of Simple Abundance' thing," you say. Maybe I am, but hear me out. When our professional lives are synchronized with our personal lives we are more apt to feel productive and essential. We sense that we are moving toward something meaningful and tangible—that we are working for more than just a paycheck. We have purpose and a sense of progress. We have a life.

On the other hand, when our professional lives are working against us, either negatively influencing or entirely overwhelming our personal goals, we often feel frustrated, lost, and unfulfilled—as if we are merely marking time. We become pessimists. What's a pessimist? In my book it's someone who can look at the land of milk and honey and see only calories and cholesterol. As pessimists, we drift along toward personal substantiation but absent a true connection to a living blueprint, we over-indulge in what gratification we can find through our work. Living almost one-dimensionally, our identities center on positions, titles, and professional responsibilities. If that's happiness, it's of the artificial variety.

As we move further away from our personal agendas and closer to artificial happiness, superficial measurements of success become confused with fulfilling ones and we over-identify with "things" measured monetarily or materialistically. Who we are becomes secondary to what we do, what we have, and what we earn. This is the ultimate negation of our humanity.

> *"First say to yourself what you would be; and then do what you have to do."*
>
> — Epictetus

The blueprint that I ultimately created for my own life did include a number of professional objectives. However, this time, and for the first time, I looked at work as supplementary to my life's plan rather than as primary. Making money and professional success were still very important, but they were not all-important. That's something for a guy like me—a guy who considered himself a provider first, and a parent, partner, and person, second.

The next step was to break down the objectives of my plan into daily, weekly, and monthly activities that, when accomplished, would move me directly toward the achievement of a larger goal. My action plan looked like any business or sales plan except that it also contained a calendar of activities that supported the numbers, rather than just numbers. Presented this way, my plan fit exactly into my method for managing time and promised some kind of balance between my personal and my professional lives. Now, all I had to do was execute the plan.

Here's where it went to hell. Sunday's plan became Monday's folly as unforeseen obstacles became all too visible. The harder I tried to make the plan work the greater the rebuff I felt. The faster I ran, the sooner the obstacles overwhelmed me. My agenda evaporated before my eyes, taking my enthusiasm, confidence, and determination with it.

Defeated and more than slightly humiliated, I looked even deeper into my psyche in hope of finding a solution or at least a reasonable explanation. Aware of my tendency to cast blame outward when things go wrong, I forced myself—no easy task—to accept complete responsibility for my failure and to review the entire planning process clinically rather than emotionally.

This approach yielded immediate dividends. Upon examination, the plan that I created was so tightly wound that there was no room for contingencies. Unable to fight a war on two fronts and manage the plan while dealing with issues that I hadn't considered, I had become imprisoned by my own escape plan.

Naïvely believing that discipline and determination would carry the day, I had also neglected to recognize and appreciate the need to remain flexible with my expectations of others. Additionally, I had failed to consider the impact of unpredictable interruptions, annoyances, and putting out the daily "fires" that consistently disrupted my schedule and my sense of well being. Finally, I had to realize that any expectation of perfection was ridiculous and self-defeating. After all, I had never seriously attempted this type of planning before. Why on earth I anticipated complete mastery of the process the first time out is beyond me—but I did.

Appropriately humbled, I tried again. The results were only slightly better, but I was now willing to settle for progress rather than perfection. Adopting diligence as my mantra, I stayed with it—regrouping and adjusting as circumstances dictated. Days turned to weeks and weeks to months and I stayed the course, gradually recognizing that progress was being made and rejoicing at the fact that I was closer to accomplishing my goals than I had ever been before. Months turned into years and I have never looked back.

> *"Everything you put in your way is just a method of putting off the hour when you could actually be doing your dream. You don't need endless time and perfect conditions. Do it now. Do it today. Do it for twenty minutes and watch your heart start beating."*
>
> — Barbara Sher

Today I am able to manage setbacks and false starts with relative ease, and I view them for what they really are—changes that I need to make. I have become much more tolerant and accepting of other peoples' rights to be human and imperfect. Remember that "impatient child waiting for the party" from earlier in this chapter? Well, I'm not cured yet, but I have learned to enjoy the anticipation of the achievement almost as much as the achievement itself.

Coming full circle to the original point I made about people being intimidated by my list of personal and professional objectives, the fact is that they don't know what I know—that I can do it, that I can make my plan reality. So can you.

Before you begin sculpting your plan, consider these thoughts:

Stuff happens. Good, bad, and indifferent, it happens. If you are counting on perfect plan execution and your expectations for a successful outcome are connected to a rigid timeline, you are looking at a "DefCon 5" level plan failure. Effective planning requires flexibility and perspective. Think for a moment about a professional football team preparing for a Sunday game. The coaches, staff, and players spend the entire week creating and practicing a game plan that is based upon all of the available information that they have regarding their opponent. What happens the minute the game begins? The plan begins to change and continues to change throughout the game. Adjustments are made based upon new information received and unanticipated circumstances such as injury, weather, and the score. To enter the game without the initial plan would be folly, as would it be foolishly stubborn not to alter it along the way. An adaptability to change is needed of all plans, including your plan. Be patient, look for the unforeseen and make adjustments as necessary. Treat it as a true work in progress and you will arrive at your objective … but rarely according to the original plan. Even small changes can reap big results. Think of a sea captain, who knows that there are many forces that control the movement of a giant ship in the open seas, especially in bad weather. But he also knows that turning the relatively small rudder only a degree or two can alter the destination of a ship by 1,000 miles.

Time is not on your side. Nor is it against you really; it just feels that way because it does not conform to your demands. Time does its own thing, ticks away at its own pace, and pays no attention to your agendas, sales quotas, or deadlines. Be very liberal with your expectations, particularly concerning events or people beyond your direct control. In the end, our objectives are most often achieved when the timing is right. Work diligently toward your objective and focus on the footwork, not on the clock.

Believe in yourself. If you anticipate success, you will recognize it when it comes. If you expect failure, you will find more than enough reasons to quit. Although it is natural to second-guess our decisions and doubt our abilities, we must override these insecure moments with heaping portions of self-confidence. You will not get the reassurance you need from any other source but yourself.

Others cannot and will not accept ownership for your goals, nor can they ever become emotionally attached to your success. In lieu of a fan club, we must look internally for the support that we need to carry on. When it comes to finding what we want in life, we all walk alone.

Visualize success. Surround yourself with tangible evidence of your progress and visual reminders of your objectives. I often have participants in my programs create a collage that is a pictorial representation of their individual definitions of success. They hang them in their office, they tack them up at home, they keep them in their planners, or any other place where they can be reminded, on a daily basis, why they do what they do. Many people find it valuable to make a list of their goals and review the list at least once a week to check their progress and to stay on track with their activities. Remember, the larger the objective, the greater the obstacles to achievement. Keeping your objectives in front of you at all times gives you the determination you will need when it is needed the most.

Developing A Personal Business Plan

In his book, *The Seven Habits of Highly Successful People*, author Stephen Covey suggests that all planning processes should "begin with the end in mind". As we have already reviewed, our "end" is our list of *personal objectives*. Our professional objectives are only a means to that end and are only worth doing if they are directly or indirectly contributing to our personal success. Our first step is to build our list.

Step One – Identify Some Personal Objectives:

To begin this process, start with a blank sheet of paper and write down *everything* that you have ever considered important or desirable to accomplish, acquire, or enjoy. Pay special attention to the things you used to do and no longer do, activities that you presently do, but don't do often enough, and things you have always wanted to do, but haven't found the time, the money, or the _____ (fill in the excuse) to get them done. Allow your mind to take you where it wants to go; make no immediate decisions on whether the goal can or cannot be done, or when and how it can be done; just write it all down. There is no need to prioritize at this point, nor do we need to get hung up on evaluating the merits of any one item on your list. Some goals may be as simple as doing laundry twice a week, cleaning the garage, getting to the gym, buying a new suit, being home in time for dinner, etc. Others may be lofty and complex. **All have merit.**

> *"People who say that life is not worthwhile are*
> *really saying that they themselves have no personal*
> *goals which are worthwhile."*
> — Maxwell Maltz

Next, on a separate sheet of paper, describe what your desired life would be like five years from now, both professionally and personally. Pay particular attention to where your time will be allocated and be sure to note your income level. Record as many details of the vision as possible. Spend some time here and do not rush the process—short, creative bursts are best. Don't concern yourself with writing style, spelling, or even finishing.

Finally, compare the results of each exercise. Look for similarities and specific objectives that support your vision. These are the things that will add depth and purpose to your life. These are the things that define who you are, where you are, and where you should go. These are the things that you were born to do and should live to do. These are the things that will make you happy. Now, you have to determine if you are willing to do all that is necessary to achieve them.

> *"Always bear in mind that your own resolution to*
> *succeed is more important than any other one thing."*
> — Abraham Lincoln

Assuming that you are planning to continue your pursuit of your objectives, let's move onto step two and begin to sketch out your personal business plan.

Step Two – Select Your Annual Income:

The best thing about being in sales is that you are, to a large extent, able to determine how much money you are going to make each year. Of course, you should choose an income amount that is realistic. However, guard against under-financing your personal agenda. After doing the exercises in Step One, you've likely added some additional objectives to your list (i.e. gym membership, tuition, flying lessons) that may not be in the current budget. I usually ask producers with an earnings history in the industry to target a 30% increase in production from the prior year. Your figure may be higher or lower depending on what "30%" equates to. Either way, challenge yourself to reach a new level.

> *"One way to keep momentum going is to have constantly greater goals."*
> — Michael Korda

Step Three – Identify Income-Producing Activities:

What is it going to take to achieve my income goals? Simply stated, if you intend to increase your production by 30%, then you must spend 30% more time engaged in the activity that will generate the increases. Assuming that you do not presently have 3 hours (30% x 10 hour day) of free time built into your daily schedule to spend on new activities, and understanding that any additional time spent at work will negatively impact your personal agenda, we are left with only one choice—find the efficiencies necessary to create the time required.

As we will discuss in our next chapter on Priority Management, deciding what not to do is as important as deciding what should be done. For now, we will limit our topic to those activities that will directly contribute to the achievement of our production objective, and we will assume that we will be able to make the time available.

Let's further examine what we mean by income-producing activity. In sales*, these are the actions that you take to create new business opportunities. They include:

- Marketing
- Prospecting
- Networking
- Referral Harvesting
- Cross-selling
- Client Servicing

---

* In a service position where additional income opportunities may be limited or not exist at all, you will be challenged with creating and presenting a new compensation formula that includes things like referral fees, cross-selling incentives, retention bonuses, and commission splits on new business opportunities that you bring in. I struggle to think of a single agency or carrier that I have worked with that wouldn't not only agree to this kind of request, but would welcome it.

As mentioned in the prior section, the degree to which *real* opportunity is created and converted into new business correlates directly with your ability to establish integrity-based producer-client relationships and your capacity to support these relationships with consistent value-added services.

Unfortunately, most business planning discussions pay too little regard to the proactive, service-oriented selling behaviors found in our model that carefully target and develop quality opportunities. Instead, they prefer to focus on sales strategies that use the conventional "contact, pitch, and close" approach to new business development that targets everybody. They are often inclined to this type of selling activity because the efforts usually yield short-term results that are generally assumed to be good results.

Additionally, the tactics that support the strategy are easy to quantify and easy to manage. Call quotas are established, contacts are conjectured, appointment hits are calculated, proposal estimates are formulated, and close ratios are determined to define the payoff. One hundred calls yield fifty contacts, which nets sixteen appointments that generate eight proposals that convert to one sale. It's all so mathematical. If the results are something less than desirable, increase the number of calls, go bang on doors, and "hit 'em" with direct mail.

> "The darkest hour of a man's life is when he sits down
> to plan how to get money without earning it."
> — Horace Greeley

Cross-selling, referral harvesting, networking, and channel marketing initiatives, if considered at all, are most often perceived as supplemental and too difficult to measure. Building relationships with existing clients is seen as a "service thing" and relationships with prospects are contingent upon timely progress toward a sales event. Proactive risk management and loss control programs aren't examined or considered at all. Marketing strategies in this environment are typically impersonal and sporadic rather than carefully targeted and strategically coordinated. All initiatives tend to be price- and product-driven rather than value-driven.

Whether or not this price and product formula works is irrelevant. Arguably it does work, and any successful telemarketing organization is standing evidence to this fact. Does this strategy, however, provide you with the most efficient return for your time and attention, given that it requires up to twenty times more effort, time, and money to court a new client than is required to create a new opportunity from an existing one? Is such a sales-driven, self-serving posture conducive to building lasting client relationships that identify and promote win/win opportunities? We will talk more about this in the chapter on Channel Marketing. For now, the answer to both questions is an unqualified no.

"There is no right way to do something wrong."
— unknown

If we firmly believe that our existing clients represent more than meat on a hook, and we have faith that through proactive client management we can create a limitless supply of new opportunities, then we must develop a strategy that opens the portals to these more reliable sources for new business development.

We will begin by grouping our business building tactics into four developmental areas that are supported by your *high pay-off activities*. Your high pay-off activities are defined as the actions that you initiate to build relationships with potential clients or to maintain relationships with existing clients. They include:

Marketing and Prospecting: This is the process of identifying, qualifying, and approaching targeted accounts. Our methods are focused on client and market need. Our objective is to establish in the minds of our prospects an awareness of our value and ability to provide proactive risk management and loss control services that reduce the cost of insurance over time. Our message is personalized and designed to provide our target clients with enough information to make an educated evaluation of our integrity, value, and trustworthiness. We pick our clients rather than hoping that they will pick us. We avoid the bidding process altogether. We bring only quality carriers to the table, and we walk away from accounts that are only interested in the lowest price. You are likely to lose this kind of business next year anyway. Our marketing events are synchronized and consistent, ensuring that each contact builds on the last. Our strategy is designed to attract, not to intrude, and our marketing events are not selling events. We do not make cold calls.

Presenting: Maintaining a regular and open dialogue with all clients, potential and existing, is a critical element in establishing confidence in your dependability, integrity, and responsiveness. Only through regular contact will you begin to develop an awareness of your client's specific needs, and only then will your client recognize your value to them. *Every* client contact is relevant to your marketing plan. Clients respect and respond well to producers who are predictably visible, viable, and available. Clients react negatively to hurried and harried producers who, selling the old fashioned way, have more places to be and more people to see than they can possibly squeeze into a day. Remember that their formula calls for a one-percent return for their time and attention. They have to move fast, and they have to move often. They have to hear "no" ninety-nine times before the "yes" is found. The most important element in any sale, and in establishing any relationship, has always been the rapport and the trust established at the start. The image that you create in the beginning is the one that will be remembered, so it is best to prepare well and listen even better.

Servicing: To be considered different and more valuable than other producers, you must actually do things differently and better. This means bypassing traditional insurance selling and servicing practices in favor of activities that prove your commitment to the client and that build your credibility in advance of the sale. Supporting your client relationships at the outset by providing, or offering to provide, value-added services such as loss control ideas, risk management suggestions, current policy evaluations, thorough needs assessments, and forums for client education, allows you to demonstrate your value and your commitment before an insurance decision has to be made. Additionally, you are able to assess your client's culture and insurance buying practices prior to investing the time required to find a market and formulate a proposal. By removing the sales event as a precondition for servicing your account, you are immediately established on a different and higher plane than any of your competitors.

Planning: Nothing happens unless you make it happen. Suppose you were on a non-stop flight to Tokyo and heard the following announcement: "Ladies and Gentlemen, this is your captain speaking. We're traveling west across the Pacific Ocean. In a few hours you will be able to look down and see land. When that happens we'll start looking for a big city with an airport. If we find one before our fuel runs out, we'll land. Then we'll figure out where we are and decide where we want to go next. In the meantime, relax and enjoy your flight." How can you relax when nobody has planned ahead? That's why you need a plan, specifically one that works. The strategies that we develop will require proactive and consistent delivery over time. Our process is guaranteed to bring you total success, personally and professionally, if you are committed to doing the footwork. Your plan will work if you work it or it will fail if you don't. True success does not happen accidentally nor is it a function of good fortune and circumstance. The only way to ensure success is to plan accordingly. Knowing in advance that everything that you wish to do cannot get done, you must create a plan that promises to deliver on the important stuff. What you do and when you do it will be a function of careful planning rather than on-the-spot reactions. You will do what you need to do when you need to do it and you will be where you need to be when you need to be there. Hey, as Yogi Berra once said, if you don't know where you're going you could wind up somewhere else.

Deciding which proactive selling and servicing activities to engage in is a function of preference, experience, and ability. To be effective and credible, your list of sales and service initiatives must only include activities with which you are comfortable, that you believe in, and that fit who you are.

For instance, if you are not good at public speaking, then giving workplace safety seminars should not be on your list. If you shy away from evening social gatherings due to your personal agenda, don't include them either. If you don't believe in direct mail, don't use it. Trying to be something that you are not is awkward and uncomfortable for you and your audience. Forget what other people do or think that you should do. Stick to activities and strategies that are natural and reflect who you are.

> *"It generally happens that assurance keeps an even pace with ability."*
>
> — Samuel Johnson

Here is a list of sample high-payoff activities that were developed by other successful producers and account executives. Use them as thought starters. Notice that each is proactive, service-driven, quantified, and easy to schedule.

"I will ask for two referrals per week from existing clients."

"I will host a series of quarterly workplace safety symposiums."

"I will call three clients per week just to check in."

"I will have two new business appointments per week."

"I will send out 10 pre-approach letters per week and call to follow up."

"I will meet with a carrier representative/underwriter each week for lunch."

"I will conduct an on-location visit with each client once per quarter."

"I will attend each safety committee meeting for my top ten accounts."

"I will become active with the Chamber of Commerce or Rotary and attend each scheduled meeting."

"I will establish an electronic clipping file for my target market and email copies of pertinent articles with personalized notes to clients and targets once per month."

"I will host an EPLI roundtable for new and existing clients once per quarter."

"I will write two articles per year for an industry trade journal."

"I will create and use a risk-management assessment tool for all new target clients beginning with one per week."

"I will conduct a thorough claims review with my top ten accounts once per quarter."

"I will have lunch with two clients per week."

"I will develop and distribute via e-mail an electronic risk management newsletter to my mailing list once per quarter."

"I will attend two target market industry trade shows this year."

"I will conduct bi-annual needs assessments with existing clients in an effort to locate cross selling opportunities."

Take the time right now to create your own list of sales and service activities. Your list does not have to be all-inclusive nor will it ever be complete. Like fad exercises, ideas come and go; some are good and will work; and some will not. The trick is to identify which ideas have the best chance for success prior to committing to any course of action. The only way to properly evaluate those ideas is to write them down. Write down *everything* that you would like to do or could do better. Documenting your ideas creates a menu from which you will select your key high-payoff initiatives. There's no law that's locking you into any one idea at this point so let the ideas flow.

One final thing—avoid recording activity that is routine or reactive. Answering the phone on the second ring or conducting pre-renewal meetings 60 days prior to the expiration date is not fascinating, different, or un-expected—unless you do it naked. And we don't want to go there.

> *"There is no sudden leap into the stratosphere ....*
> *There is only advancing step by step, slowly and*
> *tortuously, up the pyramid toward your goals ...."*
> — Ben Stein

These activities, or others like them, will become the foundation for our business plans. If we wish to increase production by any significant amount, and if we desire consistent, steady growth beyond the short term, we must establish a working action plan that allocates significant time to these high pay-off, new business-building activities. Time taken from these activities and given to distractions, interruptions, crises, and other unplanned activities, reduces your production and wastes tremendous amounts of energy.

Step Four – Developing *The Plan*:

Starting with your production objective (your sales goal), we'll select the activities that will become the basis of the plan for achieving that goal. Review the sample *Goal Planning Sheet* on the following page and use it as a guide while completing your own plan. We will eventually create a similar plan for your service objectives and supplemental plans for your marketing initiatives and planning time (yes, you even have to plan time for planning). A complete set of Goal Planning Sheets can be found in our Online Library. To access the library and print up your own copies of this form, go to our website at www.gopolestar.com and select "Online Library" from the menu.

Let's get started:

Development Area: Production

Today's Date:	Target Date:	Measurement:	Date Accomplished:
June 21, 2002	June 21, 2003	Agency Commissions	

Commitment Statement:

Increase my annual production by 30%, from $310,000 to $403,000 in the next year.

Specific Action Steps

Activity	Start Date	Quantity	Frequency
1. Design personalized pre-approach letter to target market hospitality program prospects. Send and follow up.	June 25	Ten	Weekly
2. Ask for referrals from existing clients.	June 25	Two	Weekly
3. Identify key associations for target and request membership and publication information. Ask for trade journals and needs assessment assistance. Write article.	July	One	Quarterly
4. Develop top 50 prospects list for target market and approach them.	August 15	Five	Weekly
5. Target industry-related networking opportunity with CPAs, lawyers and brokers. Meet for lunch.	August 15	One	Weekly
6. Host prospect & client Safety Symposium breakfast for 70 people.	August 25	One	Quarterly
7. Develop clipping file for client information and send.	August 31	Top 50	Monthly
8. Face-to-face meetings with new clients	August 31	Two	Weekly

Benefits From Achieving This Goal:

1. Vacation to Italy	2. Buy Beach House	3. Increased Job Security
4. Improved Self-Esteem	5. Promotion Opportunities	6. Maximize 401K Contribution

1) Access the Online Library. at www.gopolestar.com and print one set of Goal Planning Sheets which consists of one sample and five blank forms.

2) In the space marked "Development Area", print the word "Production".

3) Fill in the dates (we suggest an annual target date) and your planned tracking tool in the "Measurement" Section. Your measurement for stating and tracking your goal can be commissions, or personal income (which you already have determined), premium income, or number and quality of new accounts (i.e. $50,000 or more), etc.

4) Create a commitment statement in the space provided that specifically defines the objective. Ensure that the production target is quantitative and realistic.

Examples:

Poorly stated objectives	Specific and Measurable Objectives
"Increase New Business"	"Improve New Business Production by 30% in the coming year"
"Increase Income from Commissions"	"Increase Commission Income this year from $125,000 to $165,000"

(Our example illustrates a production goal with an increase of 30% as an objective.)

Next, in the section of the Goal Sheet marked *"Specific Action Steps"*, list the steps you will employ that support your objective. You will also state when to initiate the activity, and how frequently you will carry out the action. A goals program, without this type of detailed action plan to support it, is difficult to adhere to and almost impossible to administer consistently. Review your initial list of ideas and select five or six activities with which you would like to start. Remember that an effective plan is composed of specific daily, weekly, monthly, quarterly, and annual action steps that are targeted directly at the objective. When designing your plan, focus on developing new strategies and refining existing approaches to improve consistency and frequency. Make no decisions about whether the desired actions can or cannot be done, or will or will not be done. Focus only on breaking down the large objective into small manageable bites.

When selecting the start date for implementing your strategy try to overestimate the time and attention that can be consistently designated to each action item. In most cases, the action items will be new to you and will require more time than you might imagine before they develop into comfortable routines. Spreading out the implementation dates permits this "re-tooling" time and reduces the likelihood that the new strategies will prove too overwhelming to implement systematically. Do nothing in masses. New habits take time to form, and … time takes time.

List at least six benefits associated with accomplishing your objective. Why do you do what you do and continue to do it? Because it's beneficial for you, that's why. Critical to your success is selecting objectives that you are committed to, rather than just interested in. To succeed, total commitment is needed. Yet sometimes we think we're committed when we're not. A chicken and a pig were talking about commitment. The chicken said, "I'm committed to giving eggs every morning". The pig said, "Giving eggs is no commitment—it's participation. Now giving ham—*that's* total commitment". A good story and well worth remembering. Why? Because your level of commitment is determined by the degree to which you will benefit from the accomplishment of the goal. The larger the goal, the greater the payoff. If the benefits from achieving the objective outweigh the inconveniences associated with overcoming the obstacles, then you will be able to muster the compulsory determination, persistence, and creativity—in short, the commitment—to see you through. Reverse the equation, however, and you will founder. Your benefits must be clearly defined before you take any action.

Be patient. Most action plans and goal programs fail because we fail to integrate the desired action steps into our routines. Initially, we may be attempting to hold onto our old habits—going about our business as we always have while trying to add these new activities to an already filled agenda. Eventually, feeling overwhelmed, we drop the plan in favor of familiarity. When properly designed, a good system permits you to progressively inject any necessary new activities into your normal day where eventually they too can become part of your routine. As this transition occurs, non-productive behavior and habits gradually work their way out of your day to make room for the new. These changes take time (usually eight to twelve weeks) to become established, so patience and determination are critical, especially in the first few weeks.

Review your planning sheet daily and make alterations as necessary. When first developed, your action plan is a mere sketch of your intended route of travel, not the well-designed road map we sometimes wish it would be. As unforeseen obstacles develop, you should remain flexible and be willing to adopt a new approach as necessary. No plan is perfect and no event entirely predictable. Additionally, new opportunities naturally present themselves as we move along the path. Proceed without blinders and enjoy the journey.

Celebrate your victories. Major accomplishments are the result of chaining together a series of lesser achievements that occur throughout the implementation of an action plan. The simple recognition of these milestones provides the needed incentive, believability, and enthusiasm to help you continue.

> *"The person determined to achieve maximum success learns the principle that progress is made one step at a time. A house is built a brick at a time. Football games are won a play at a time. Every big accomplishment is a series of little accomplishments."*
> — David Joseph Schwartz

Your Personal Goals Program

This is a good place to step back for a moment and address the issue of money. Does our quest for financial success automatically render us shallow, greedy, corrupt and insincere? Hardly. Instead, I believe that we are sometimes assigned these labels out of envy and rage by those who are not willing to work hard to realize their own ambitions. They view our passion for prosperity as somehow unfair, as if we have been given something or we are somehow privileged. They don't acknowledge *the work;* however, our critics seem to feel equally entitled to the fruits of our labor without feeling a need to endure the labor. Hey, it's easier to criticize than analyze; less of a sweat to rationalize than to actualize. Forget people who deplore your financial standing without recognizing the hard work that got you there. They're annoying, like bubblegum on your shoe, but much easier to discard.

All I really know about money is that you have to work hard to make it, and you have to work even harder to keep it. As a result, I'm always working at one financial objective or another, and there has never been a moment in my life when I have been *completely* satisfied or content. This does not mean that I am unhappy with my progress, it simply means that I am not dead yet and I truly view "work" as an important part of my life.

> *"Those who accomplish great things ... are the ones*
> *who have faith in the money-producing power of*
> *their ideas."*
>
> — Charles Fillmore

Disclosing this truth in public often produces unsolicited recommendations for remedial treatments from people who presume me afflicted with depression, addiction, or some other malady. They mean well, but they have misinterpreted my passion for goals, particularly financial ones, as an unhealthy, narrow-minded, power-hungry fixation. When confronted in this way I try very hard to listen to the advice being offered and make note of the recommended cure for my "disorder".

Curious by nature and just a little afraid of missing something, I've taken the time to read the suggested books, listen to the masters, meditate, beat the drums, and walk the coals as advised. These exhibitions and writings are usually interesting and even occasionally compelling; however, nothing that I have experienced thus far indicates that the pursuit of "more" is unhealthy, abnormal, condemning, or to be avoided. In fact, quite the contrary seems to be true. Boiled down to their core ideas, all of these teachings are essentially communicating a common message—don't hurt each other, and make the most out of life.

The most celebrated book on the topic of accumulating wealth, and also the forerunner of self-help books for business people, Napoleon Hill's *Think & Grow Rich*, reveals the timeless "secrets" of success that were used by distinguished men of great wealth and achievement to amass their fortunes. In less than three hundred pages, Hill describes, with exactness and inspiration, a simple process for achieving any desired level of affluence. The theory behind Hill's method is that, with the exception of the mentally challenged, we are all born with everything necessary to become fully successful in all aspects of our lives.

As I understand it, we all harbor a variety of personal ambitions that are defined, qualified, and quantified in a way that is unique to each of us. These goals, which are generally categorized as our financial, spiritual, charitable, educational, material, and social objectives, can coexist in perfect harmony with each other, receive equal priority, and be entirely achievable, providing that we meet and maintain the following conditions:

1) We formally (in writing) identify and quantify our objectives.
2) We create a plan of action to accomplish the objectives.
3) We believe in our ability to accomplish the objectives.
4) We believe that we should accomplish the objectives.
5) We work actively to accomplish the objectives.

Actualizing our wildest dreams then, is merely a matter of following this simple formula. Identify what you want; build a plan to achieve it, and discipline yourself to follow the plan. Not a terribly complicated idea and, in fact, right in line with the ideas that we put forth in our Business Planning Section. Why then do so many people fail to ever realize their fullest potential? Why are so many people so easily dissuaded from reaching for the stars? Why is it so common to settle for less at the expense of all that is possible? Simple as our formula might be to comprehend, it appears anything but easy to carry out.

"No more effort is required to aim high in life,
to demand abundance and prosperity, than is
required to accept misery and poverty."
— Napoleon Hill

After talking to several thousand men and women, Hill identified thirty-one major causes for failure. Chief among them was "lack of a well-defined purpose in life". He states: "There is no hope of success for the person who does not have a central purpose, or a definite goal at which to aim. Ninety-eight out of every hundred of those whom I have analyzed had no such aim." Next on his list, Hill points to a "lack of ambition to aim above mediocrity" as a common cause for failing to become successful. The prognosis for these people is dismal as well. "We offer no hope for the person who is so indifferent as to not want to get ahead in life." It follows then that most people are underachievers who have failed to utilize their latent talent and consistently under-value their true worth. Those of us who know what we want and have a burning desire to achieve it then, truly are extraordinary people; not *because* of our ability, but merely because we *use* our ability.

It has never been easier than it is today to be "mediocre"—to settle in and settle for less. With just a modicum of effort most people can comfortably get by in school, in work, at home, and in life without ever stepping up to accept a serious challenge or take a serious risk. In fact, we have created such a culture of conformity that most dreams fall dead not from a lack of ability, but out of respect for what is considered standard and customary. Early in life we are taught the importance of fitting in, and in everything we are trained to conform our behavior to one convention or the other. Fearing ridicule and disrepute, we too easily accept our prescribed limitations, render our wildest dreams unreachable, and revise our agenda for living so that it corresponds to what others deem acceptable and normal. We then become a product of our influences rather than an outgrowth of our God-given talents. In short, we learn our *place* at the expense of our *calling* and we are conditioned to keep it.

> *"Your world is a living expression of how you are*
> *using and have used your mind."*
> — Earl Nightingale

Fortunately or unfortunately, our soulful dreams and accompanying talents never completely give way. Fortunately, for those of us who shake off the narrow-minded confines of mediocrity and dare to realize our full potential. Unfortunately, for those who live by a majority rule in a society governed by internal conflict, insecurity, and emotional friction. The unfortunates are soul-sick. They are also the largest segment of our population and they angrily justify their indolence by criticizing that which is contrary to their limited point of view. Like anything extraordinary, we stand out in a crowd—and make easy targets.

> *"Keep away from people who try to belittle your*
> *ambitions. Small people always do that, but the really*
> *great make you feel that you too can become great."*
> — Mark Twain

Now, about the money. There is, of course, an undeniable truth in the aphorism that "money can't buy you happiness". We should also note that money can't buy you misery either. Neither of these emotions are for sale. In fact, money can't buy you *any* emotional condition unless, of course, it is used to purchase a mood- or mind-altering drug. Still, money certainly seems to *bring* happiness to people. Franklin D. Roosevelt said that happiness "lies in the joy of achievement". Money is also a by-product of achievement, so it is reasonable to expect that achievement could yield both happiness and money. Difficult though it may be for the cynic and pessimist to accept, money and happiness are very closely connected. There is nothing immoral or unethical about your desire for wealth and prosperity. There is nothing immoral about wanting more than you presently have if you are willing to work for it.

Working toward an established income objective then, regardless of what others think of your goal, does not spoil your integrity, does not make you shallow, does not mean that you are greedy, bigoted, lack spirituality, or are Scrooge-like. On the flip side, gauze robes, new-age music, long hair, and sandals are not necessary for one to be spiritually connected and socially sensitive. Just self-satisfied, from what I can tell. So why, in the face of this wisdom, must we contend with all of the jealousies, judgments, righteousness, and labeling that successful people often endure? It's because successful people are "different". And as Arthur Godfrey used to say, "If you are the only petunia in an onion patch, you are going to draw attention."

Successful people choose to be individual rather than invisible, and they do not disguise who they are or what they desire. After all, clichés, generalizations, and stereotypes are the fabrications of the ignorant and insecure. Personally, I am relieved to discover that making money is not only acceptable, it is very much encouraged. Actually, this is good news for anybody who sells for a living. It is one of my favorite things to do, and, I believe, it always will be.

> "... I learned this at least, by my experiment; that
> if one advances confidently in the direction of his
> dreams, and endeavors to live the life which he has
> imagined, he will meet with success unexpected in
> common hours."
> — Henry David Thoreau, *On Walden Pond*

Why did you choose to sell for a living? I think it is because you are smart. Smart enough to realize that your destiny is your decision and not a forgone conclusion. Smart enough, and bold enough, to accept responsibility for your financial success and to select a profession that has limitless income potential. Smart enough to follow your dreams rather than contain them or ignore them.

> *"No pessimist ever discovered the secrets of the stars, sailed to uncharted land, or opened a new heaven to the human spirit."*
> — Hellen Keller

Pay no attention to the mindless musings of the masses who contend that great personal wealth either cannot be had legitimately or should be avoided morally. Those who settle for less are not settling for something better, and they certainly are in no position to judge you or your ambitions. You and God together are adequately positioned and qualified enough to evaluate your potential, to determine the worthiness of your objectives, and to measure your life's progress. Everybody else is just making noise.

The twin afflictions of melancholy and malaise have reached epidemic proportions in our world, robbing us of talent and destroying generations of evolutionary and economic advancement. If you want to be free and to prosper, steer a wide berth away from negative people, stay inoculated to cynicism, be true to yourself, and go with your plan. Make as much money as you want, make more than you need, and make it without guilt. You are worth it. Your soul knows your own truth, and it knows your value. Trust it and pay attention.

Here are some thoughts to consider before you finalize your personal action plan:

> God does not make trash. Nobody is supposed to live a life of misery and hardship and everybody has an inherent ability to prosper. The only requirement for becoming affluent is deciding to do so, and we, ourselves, are the greatest obstacle that we will encounter. True, bad things do happen to good people and sometimes there is no avoiding the poison. However, do not ever confuse failing with being a failure. To fail at something or to make a mistake, particularly with something new and untried, is a perfectly natural consequence of trying. Learn what you can from every setback and move on without regret.

> Poverty is not glamorous. The starving artist, no matter how romantically portrayed, is painting to eat. He is also decaying physically, he is nutritionally deprived, and he is otherwise depressed. There is a reason the Turn-on, Tune-in, Drop-out generation went back to work—it's called Winter.

Greed is not good. However, desire, ambition, and ability all coming together with a willingness to work, is wonderful. To be good at something and get paid for it, regardless of the amount, is not greedy. It is only an indication that something of value has been exchanged for money. It is the way the world works and it is the way the world should work. Financial success is often assumed to be a product of greed because of a mistaken belief that somebody has gotten more than his or her share. There are no shares. Affluence is limitless.

It's never easy. Otherwise everybody would do it. Success in sales, and the monetary rewards that come with it, is the result of consistent and disciplined high pay-off activity over time. It is hours, days, weeks, months, and years of hard work and diligence. It is long stretches of rejection and misfires that are occasionally interrupted by a revitalizing Yes. It is crowded planes, loud hotels, late nights, and early mornings. It is lonely at the top, miserable at the bottom, and disquieting in between. There are no gimmies; we earn our right to do what we do and we deserve every cent that we make.

Be proud of what you do. You did not settle for a job, you selected an opportunity. You are self-empowered to create your own future, and you are committed to becoming successful—both professionally and personally. It doesn't matter whether or not your work is fashionable or popular—you have the stuff from which legends are made. Honor yourself and your heritage—always do work that you are proud of.

> *"Every human being who reaches the age of understanding of the purpose of money wishes for it. Wishing will not bring riches. But desiring riches with a state of mind that becomes an obsession, then planning definite ways and means to acquire riches, and backing those plans with persistence which does not recognize failure, will bring riches."*
>
> — Napoleon Hill

Creating Your Personal Goals Program

Many of us have been told to keep our private lives and our professional lives separated. Disciples of this "don't mix business with pleasure" theory suggest that by blocking thoughts of one while engaged in the other, we become more focused and more productive in both. In reality, however, such a black and white approach to life is inappropriate and counter-productive to building a solid foundation upon which we can achieve our dreams and aspirations.

Our profession is what we do, not who we are, and we do it to facilitate a standard of living from which we define the meaning of our existence. If you completed the benefits exercise and created your list and your vision of the future, you will notice that most, if not all of the benefits associated with the professional accomplishments are personal in nature. Our lives, both professionally and personally, are not black and white, but instead cover the complete spectrum of colors. Recognize this interdependency and work with it rather than attempting to combat it. You will ultimately achieve a sense of balance, perspective, purpose, and direction that will prove more fulfilling than might presently seem possible. You can and will "have it all"—just not all at once.

Creating a personal goals program mandates that we take the time to write down our objectives and formulate a detailed plan of action (sound familiar?). A few decades back, Yale University conducted a study on a group of recent graduates. After asking who among the group had taken the time to write out their plans for the future, they determined that 3% of the graduates had such a written plan while the remaining 97% held only a conceptual idea of what the future should look like. Yale decided to track the group's progress for a thirty-year period and at the end of the study they determined that the 3% who had started with a written plan were more financially successful than the other 97% combined. This being a scientific study, Yale looked for other contributing factors (such as family wealth, academic achievement, etc.,) and could find no other correlation.

You are no different from these students. What worked for them will work for you and anybody like you who has decided to be more, do more, and have more.

To begin the development of a personal goals program, select two or three Goal Planning Sheets from the set that you printed from the library and follow the same procedure that we used when we developed your business building strategies. Your development areas may include any of the following or you may prefer to select others.

Sample Personal Development Areas:

- *Health*	- *Education*	- *Travel*	- *Investment*
- *Time Management*	- *Motivation*	- *Spirituality*	- *Family*
- *Financial*	- *Career*	- *Recreation*	- *Housing*
- *Esteem*	- *Balance*	- *Serenity*	- *Love*

When you created your list of important achievements, acquisitions, and enjoyments, you probably came up with at least one objective for each of these areas. Select only a limited number of crystallized goals to work with at one time to avoid objective overload. Our mutual goal is to understand and implement the process. There will be ample opportunity to expand your personal goals program once this is accomplished, so please be patient.

> *"No man, for any considerable period, can wear*
> *one face to himself, and another to the multitude,*
> *without finally getting bewildered as to which may*
> *be true."*
> — Nathaniel Hawthorne

Achieving what you want out of life can be as simple as defining it, believing in it, and disciplining yourself to go and get it. People are successful because at some point in their lives they decided to be successful. You must make the same decision. It is not an easy one, because the road to success is indeed the one less traveled. Ours is not a world filled with people and societies that encourage individual achievement. It is much easier to stick with the herd and adopt a herd mentality.

Our victories are often uncelebrated and our journeys frequently solitary. Successful people are quite different from the norm. And, because you are different, you must do things differently. Your decisions about what to do and what not to do should primarily depend on the degree to which the outcome will propel you toward or away from your objectives. You will not be imprisoned by the fears and limiting beliefs of others. Often you will stand alone, apart from the crowd and shielded from the distractions of life that captivate and entertain the masses. Your focus and intensity will sometimes be perceived as arrogance, intolerance, and social apathy—you will be often be labeled as anti-something. Despite the criticisms, stick to your agenda, work your plan, be true to yourself and enjoy the journey. This is an exciting world—there's a lot to be done—go and do.

> *"The only true measure of success is the ratio between what we might have done and what we might have been on the one hand, and the thing we have made and the thing we have made of ourselves on the other."*
>
> — H.G. Wells

Added Suggestions:

Take some time to visualize your success.

Create a collage—using cut out pictures, your own drawings, or any other means of representation you like—to illustrate your individual definition of the success you are seeking. You may have a collection of smiling faces to symbolize a happy family or a picture of a passport to indicate travel; use whatever images are meaningful to you. Hang your collage in your office or keep it in your daily planner as a reminder of why you do what you do. Keep your objectives—in words or pictures or both—in front of you at all times; having your goals in sight will give you the determination you need when you need it the most.

Keep a daily journal. Record your thoughts, your dreams, your ups, your downs, and your day-to-day stuff. Keeping a constant flow going from mind to hand to paper stimulates creativity and gets rid of the clutter that builds up in our conscious mind. It doesn't even matter what your write, draw, or scribble. Filling a journal page each morning gives you a clear perspective and allows you to mentally and emotionally prepare for the day. Or you may wish to journal at night to bring closure to the day. I journal each morning and each night to get the benefits of both. You might think "of course *you* do, you are the one making the suggestion". Believe me, I don't do it for show. If it didn't do anything for me, I'd deep-six it in a minute.

Exercise! What ever might be wrong with you—physically, mentally, or spiritually—can be diminished or eliminated by getting up and getting active. If you have too much stress in your life, exercise is the best way to get rid of it. When I run each day, (here he goes again … goody-two-shoes) I start the run with a bag full of bad stuff—stress, anger, frustration, annoyance, etc. By the time I'm done, most of it has been left on the pavement. You can walk, run, skip rope, bike, skate, box, lift, yoga, and a thousand other things. Just make one of them yours and make it a habit. Do something, even if it's a little something, everyday. Also, try **hitting something!** A few years ago I started working out on a heavy-bag and immediately recognized the therapeutic value of beating it up a few times a week. Best of all, it doesn't hit back.

Do something artsy. You have a creative fire that needs light and air to sustain itself. Pick up that forgotten instrument, paint brush, sketch pad, writer's pen, tutu, or sewing kit and express yourself. Living up to your full potential should not be limited to your work or your daily tasks. Set aside some time to acknowledge and explore your passions and possibilities that are too often written off as frivolous pursuits. Remember, talents that are within you are gifts that need recognition and engagement.

Chapter Four

Priority Management

"Set priorities for your goals.... A major part of successful living lies in the ability to put first things first. Indeed, the reason most major goals are not achieved is that we spend our time doing second things first."

— Robert J. McKain

Speed. We are consumed by it. We want what we want when we want it and we want to get where we're going as quickly as possible. Coincidental delays such as traffic, long lines, and late flights spark palpitations, frustration, and feelings of stagnation. Delays caused directly by someone or something that we can identify and assign responsibility to, send us over the edge.

What's the big rush? Why is where we are going next so often more important than where we are now? Why are we the only species on the planet that insists on moving faster than the rate which nature intended? Why does it take a weekend or a vacation to slow us down long enough to appreciate a walk, study a sunset, relax with a hobby, or simply have a meaningful conversation? Why? Because we have been groomed to expect instant gratification and overnight accomplishments. We have been taught that sooner is always better, success is a competitive sport, and that being first means not being left out. Far too often we are functioning on the belief that we are not where we should be—not far enough ahead, too far behind, or on the wrong path all together. So, we hustle.

Today, we seem to be driving, flying, and running about as fast as we can. Although it may be physically possible to move faster, congested highways and overloaded flyways render the speed that we currently have available unusable.

That's why we've re-directed our focus on speed, expending vast amounts of resources and energy on improving the speed of information and communication in our daily lives. So insatiable is our quest for faster transmissions and processing times that *our era* is already called the "information age" where data speeds are as much a commodity as widgets or waffles and where speed isn't measured in rpms but in bits and bytes. Technology is advancing so quickly that we, the ordinary users, hardly have time to learn about the latest innovation before the next generation comes along and renders our version obsolete quicker than a Pedro Martinez fastball. That scenario leaves us feeling like we're always a step behind Silicon Valley.

As astonishing as the rate of technological advancements may be, it's effectiveness is tempered somewhat by our inability to absorb and process endless streams of information while functioning efficiently and rationally in the new economy that is being created in its wake.

The ancient Chinese had it right when they said "may you live in interesting times...", although that's a double-edged sword. While the 21st century is surely an exhilarating time to be alive, it is also a terribly busy and often confusing time. In our hurly-burly rush to get ahead and stay ahead, we sometimes fail to recognize that one of the greatest downsides to our technological advancement is that it gives us "more" than we can handle. More information, more to do, more options, more to do, more accessibility, more to do, more to read, more to do, more to see, ...

If you still harbor the illusion that you will some how, some day, "get it all done", I have some bad news for you. You can't. I know because I've tried. But you can get the important stuff done—if you prioritize. As Henry David Thoreau said, "Read the best books first, because you won't have time to read them all." Thus, time management always means prioritizing choices. The good news is that we have a choice. The challenge is to make good choices.

> *"I am the master of my fate; I am the captain of my soul."*
> — William Ernest Henley

Compounding Choices

When I was growing up, watching television meant choosing between three channels on an old black & white Zenith in our basement. Our ratio of selection to choices available was 33%, meaning that our decision to watch one channel in lieu of the other two covered 1/3 of the available options. Today, things are a bit more complicated. My children, faced with the same decision, must select from among a hundred or more channels, countless videos, an Xbox™, or the myriad internet options. Ultimately, their selection represents a tiny percentage of the available choices. The skills required to-day to make a good decision are significantly more advanced in the amount of knowledge needed and in the ability to process that information. It is not surprising then that so many of us feel overwhelmed, scattered, and per-plexed, prone to short attention spans and a hesitancy to make decisions.

We were groomed in a different era and our "selection dexterity" is probably not as current as it needs to be. Understanding that we need to update our priority management system and upgrade our aptitude for mak-ing choices are critical first steps toward managing time from a proper and realistic perspective.

> *"Your world is a living expression of how you are using and have used your mind."*
> — Earl Nightingale

Going "E" – Blessing or Curse?

The technological breakthroughs that have occurred in this informa-tion age have made our lives much more comfortable and convenient. Mo-bile this and wireless that provide us with around-the-clock access to almost any information that we desire, dramatically improving our efficiency and availability. What was once a full day of running errands can now be con-densed into a few hours of working online. We have direct deposit paydays, electronic airline tickets, cars that rent themselves, and dry cleaners that come to your desk. We have e-conferences, e-books, e-cards, e-mail, voice-mail, fax-mail, and same-day delivery for the really bulky stuff. All of these faceless encounters are designed with your busy schedule in mind; designed to speed your day along and ostensibly give you more free time.

It's no different in the insurance industry. The tools of our trade have advanced so efficiently that we have also become nearly completely acces-sible to our clients. We can reach almost anybody and in turn be reached from virtually anywhere in the world. Vacationing in the mountains? No reason to miss e-mail—just pop open your wireless Palm Pilot. Sailing off Tahiti? Lucky you—and that fax machine on board can get you that contract requiring your signature. This enhanced ability to communicate and to gather information has, for many of us, created such a world of knowledge that we are now far more up-to-date and efficient than ever before. We can get our continuing education credits online, access industry news in seconds, create and send newsletters, and stay in constant communication with our clients and our office. New applications and online signatures have greatly expanded our ability to complete entire insurance transactions over the internet in real time. From application and submission to payment and policy issuance—no postage, no house calls.

What do we do with our "found" time? We just create more "stuff" to do, don't we? Consequently, we surrender our newly gained ground by filling the time with new activities, which gives us more to manage, more to schedule, more to worry about, more to forget, and so on. Like hamsters on a wheel in our cages, we're no further ahead and are as overwhelmed as ever.

I'm not disparaging technology—there's no question that advancements in technology have reaped a bountiful harvest, including an inexhaustible inventory of options for allocating our time and attention. Unfortunately, our available time has not increased to meet the demand. We still have the same 24-hour day. We find ourselves stretched beyond limits, trying desperately to fulfill every expectation, answer every call, attend every meeting, make it to the dentist, fit in breakfast, and get our karate-taking, braces-needing, horseback-riding, dancing prodigy to piano lessons on time.

It's a chaotic existence that will become even more chaotic if we do not aggressively develop a more disciplined and deliberate process for establishing our priorities and allocating our time. Those of us over the age of 12 need to recognize that old skill sets that rely on legacy thinking are too slow, too elementary, and too limiting to manage effectively in this new economy. If all of our advances are utilized to the extent for which they were designed, then our electronic gadgetry will be instrumental in this effort. Access to more and better information leads to better educated decisions. Better decisions lead to better opportunities and better opportunities lead to greater success. However, that success won't materialize unless we keep pace with technology and learn to creatively apply the tools that we are given. This requires us all to develop a new appreciation for re-education and personal adaptation. It means we learn to change when change is called for and we learn to let go of old habits, behaviors, and assumptions that are no longer appropriate.

"We grow because we struggle, we learn, and overcome."
— R.C. Allen

Technology has forever altered the way we do business and redefined what it means to work smart. Significant as these applications appear to be today, they represent only a tiny fraction of what the actual impact will be in just a few years. I once heard Bill Gates say, "we've only seen the tip of the iceberg when it comes to technology". He was right, but we can have all the technology in the world and it won't matter if we don't know how to use it or how to make the time to use it properly. If we stay smart and embrace the change, we will learn and we will benefit from each advancement (with the possible exception of cloning). If we don't ... then we won't.

Critics of the technological evolution fear that "web-enabling" the client/ producer relationship will depersonalize the sales and service environment by reducing, or even eliminating, the need for face-to-face contact. While this scenario will develop for producers who prefer to "fly the desk", smart producers and account executives will use the enhanced efficiency of technology to provide an even greater focus on personalized client relationships. By reducing the time spent on processing, administration, communication, and information gathering, these folks have more time available to spend with their clients than ever before.

More on that from Gates. In his book, *Business @ the Speed of Thought*, Bill Gates states, "It's not a matter of either-or. People think it is the cold screen vs. the warm face-to-face and assume that the person-to-person interaction will win. Because they do not see where the internet belongs on the marketing-sales-service spectrum, they underestimate the internet's capabilities.

"You want to move pure transactions to the internet, use online communication for information sharing and routine communication, and reserve face-to-face interaction for the activities that add the most value."* For us, that means to do our business electronically whenever possible, and build our relationships in person.

> *"Let our advance worrying become advance thinking and planning."*
> — Winston Churchill

The fact that technological advancement has revolutionized every aspect of our lives is not a new phenomenon. Human history has always been about innovation, evolution, and change. Consider Christopher Columbus, who changed the world not as much by his "discovery" of America, but

---

*Business @ the Speed of Thought, page 109.

through his use of the magnetic compass, which allowed ships to stray from the safety of the coast line. Or five centuries later Fred Smith, founder of Federal Express. As a student at Yale in 1965, Smith wrote a paper on his idea of a new company that would deliver business packages overnight (he got a "C" on the report). What is new at the dawn of the 21st century, however, is the speed at which these changes are occurring. Technology has always been *autocatalytic*, meaning that new inventions and advancements make it possible to generate even greater technologies by recombination. The process speeds up at a rate that increases with time, because the process catalyzes, or stimulates, its own growth.

Speed is so prevalent in the development of new technologies that if you don't like a new palmtop or laser printer, you only have to wait a week or so for a better product to roll off the assembly line. In his book, *Guns, Germs and Steel,* social anthropologist Jared Diamond observes that, "Human technology developed from the first stone tools in use two and half million years ago to the 1996 laser printer that replaced my already outdated 1992 laser printer that was used to print this manuscript. The rate of development was undetectably slow at the beginning, when hundreds of thousands of years passed with no discernable change …. Today, technology advances so rapidly that it is reported in the daily newspapers." *

Like it or not, our technology is going to continue to progress exponentially and have a considerable impact on your business. Whether or not you want it, agree with it, or believe in it—you must learn it and you must use it if you intend to manage your life effectively and efficiently. There are still those that stubbornly hang onto the false hope that they can get by without a computer and an internet connection. They point to the DotCom crash and claim victory, reason enough to avoid the ecommerce fad. They openly scorn email, cell phones, and, the worst of the worst—voice mail. They have fond memories of the busy executive that still finds the time to answer the phone every time it rings. They like paper and lots of it. They euphorically recall the "good old days" and portray them as better days. They can be stubborn, crotchety, bitter, and, like a pedestrian on the turnpike, very much in the way. They're also fearful of technology, intimidated by its power and propensity to change things dramatically. Like all skeptics that have gone before them, they too will pass.

*Guns, Germs and Steel, page 260.

*"Growth means change and change involves risks,
stepping from the known to the unknown."*
— George Shinn

Protecting Your Time

We devote a tremendous amount of attention to protecting our money, our loved ones, and our property. We try hard not to cause distress to someone else by our failure to make responsible decisions in a timely way. We study our investments carefully, purchase alarm systems, shop wisely, squander little, and save judiciously. Society has created laws to protect us from fraud and deception, which help to safeguard our financial security. Yet, unknowingly, we often allow our most valuable and least available asset, our time, to go unprotected. We permit interruptions and allow the priorities of others to over-ride our own. At work, we hesitate before delegating to an assistant, concerned more with his or her schedule than with our own. We equate customer service with response time and react too often on impulse to any client request instead of scheduling a reply at a logical time.

*"Too many people are thinking of security instead
of opportunity."*
— James F. Byrnes

Too often we put our own priorities on hold while we deal with an endless chain of issues, crises, conversations, and demands that contribute nothing to our personal or professional agenda. In the name of work, responsibility, service, dedication, and friendship we regularly take it on the chin, hoping to catch up at some point and get to the important stuff. A typical morning in this environment might look like this:

You have set aside the morning to put the finishing touches on a proposal that is due tomorrow and then the telephone rings. On the line is your largest account with a list of questions regarding the last statement. You stop what you are doing to investigate. Meanwhile, you are interrupted again by a request to attend an impromptu sales meeting at which you learn that the pipeline is insufficient and that you are to provide a list of your top prospects and the current status of each by noon. You return to your desk to find four messages; two are from prospects that you have been targeting for months. Mid-way through the first phone call you remember that your assistant's annual review is due tomorrow and you have an appointment to have the car inspected during lunch. Equal measures of frustration and anxiety creep into your psyche. The worst part? It's only 9:30 in the morning.

And so it may go, day after day, week after week. Always playing catch up, always juggling demands, always bracing yourself for the next crisis. Long days and late nights leading to frustration, stress, and an awful feeling of spinning out of control. Clearly, it is time to make some changes.

The volatility of your workday can never be completely eliminated, but its negative impact can be minimized if we take some corrective action to better protect and value our time. With a few remedial changes, we can learn to exercise our right to control what can be controlled, establish some firm boundaries around the interruptions we are willing to tolerate, and understand that personal success is a derivative of getting things done—not everything, just the important things.

> *"You are the product of your environment. So choose the environment that will best develop you toward your objective. Analyze your life in terms of its environment. Are the things around you helping you towards success—or are they holding you back?"*
>
> — W. Clement Stone

Time is our most valuable possession. The Greek philosopher Theophrastus said that "time is the most valuable thing a man can spend". And that was over 2,000 years ago. He understood that time is the measure of our existence on this earth, and the decisions that we make about how to allocate our time ultimately determine the quality and usefulness of our stay here. Clockwise, things haven't changed in 2000 years. We start each day with the same block of 24 hours, and it elapses at exactly the same rate for all of us. What we do with each moment will inevitably decide our destiny. The greatest difference between achievement and failure can be attributed to the caliber of these time allocation decisions. You don't have to be a Greek philosopher to understand that.

We make better decisions when we keep in mind that time is a frozen asset, that you cannot bargain or position for more and you can certainly waste what you have been given. When you lose it you can never get it back. Consequently, we make even better decisions when we also exercise our right to protect the time that we have and accept complete responsibility for using it productively.

"I know that no one can really stop me but myself
and that really no one can help me but myself ...,"
— Peter Nivio Zarlenga

Balancing Priorities

What makes a winner? Organization and planning, mostly. Top producers and account executives got where they are, and stay where they are, because of their ability to establish aggressive performance objectives, create a plan to achieve the objectives, and remain solidly grounded in the high-payoff activities that support the plan. Their high-payoff activities take priority and are consistently done ahead of all others. Work, or any other activity, is ranked by its ability to move them in the direction of their accomplishments and their personal and professional objectives. Distractions that cater to comfort, personal preference, or temporary pleasure are success killers that they avoid. The greater the objectives, the more time they will allocate to the process of achieving them and the more strategic their priority management system becomes. They keep first things first by mastering a balanced commitment to their personal and professional agendas. With their priorities firmly established and their action plan in place, top performers are incredibly efficient and usually wind up allocating more time, not less, to the development of their family, their community, and their company.

It seems so easy, but this is the part that causes so much anguish for the rest of us. We get so caught up in the crisis of the moment or in helping others satisfy their short term needs, that we completely lose sight of our purpose and our goals. We postpone doing what is important in favor of what is popular and then delude ourselves into believing that someday, maybe tomorrow, the time for us will come. Little by little, we can devalue our own agendas to such a degree that we end up with much less than we deserve.

Without recognizing any obvious signs, we can work endlessly and tirelessly at the wrong things for the wrong reasons and never unlock our true potential or experience real success. Talk about a recipe for disaster. The good news is that we have options. We can be controlled or we can control. We can choose our lifestyle or we can have it chosen for us.

> *"When you take charge of your life, there is no longer need to ask permission of other people or society at large … when you ask permission, you give someone veto power over your life."*
> — Geoffry F. Abert

My wife reminds me so I'll remind you: our profession is only what we do, it is not who we are. We do what we do to facilitate a standard of living from which we define the quality of our existence. We all sell different things to different people in different ways; however, we all do it for the same reason—personal gain. Work is not a hobby. It is a means to an end. It makes a world of sense to work hard and passionately, to do your best, and to push yourself to realize your full potential. But it makes no sense if your efforts come at the expense of your health, your family, or your enjoyment of simply being alive.

We've all heard the joke about the businessman who died and had engraved on his headstone "He never missed a meeting". To me it's no joke. When we finally shed this moral coil, as they say, nobody is going to want such an epitaph on their headstone. But why do so many of us live our lives like we do? Clearly, we need to strike a balance between our competing priorities in order to truly prosper, in order to really experience the life that we are entitled to.

As much as anybody, I understand how difficult it is to manage a client base, a profession, a home and family, and a social life while at the same time taking care of oneself physically, emotionally, and spiritually. As a child of the 60s, when three TV channels were plenty and the New York Yankees were the only villains on my horizon, I had yet to learn how complicated life would become. Today I know how fast it moves, and I know how tough it is to keep pace with the rate of change.

So how to keep pace? Inherently, this means doing more of some things and doing less of others. Balance demands that we take control of our behavior and focus on the productive stuff while eliminating or minimizing the time spent on the unrewarding stuff. Balance requires us to take a step back, review our options, identify and give priority to those things that give us the greatest return for our time and attention. Spelling this out so *deliberately* may seem a bit trite to you, however, you would be amazed at how easily we can seduce ourselves into believing that whatever we are doing at the moment must be important—otherwise we wouldn't be doing it.

Who hasn't cut their lawn *just so* or agonized over a big game on TV? In the scheme of things, who cares? The important thing is to stay in balance. Why? Because balance necessitates smaller sacrifices for larger gains—short-term pain for long-term gain. To be in balance means being less—less impulsive, less accommodating, and less fearful. To be in balance also means being more—more patient, more disciplined, and more caring of ourselves.

> *"Return to the root and you will find the meaning …."*
> — Sengstan

Sadly, balance is something desired by many but achieved by too few. This realization is astonishing when we recognize that when we are born, we are in a state of perfect balance. Our priorities are crystal clear (eat, sleep, stay warm, etc.) and, for all but the most unfortunate, these needs are easily met. The fact that life becomes so much more complicated as we grow up does not alter the reality that we are built for balance, and it is we who cause the imbalance.

We, meaning mankind, working outside the boundaries of nature, are responsible for creating our own chaos and friction. A disrupted personal or professional state is not an instinctive or natural one; it is one that we create and adopt. Nature prefers harmony.

I hate to sound like another circle-of-life, live and let live, granola-crunching, Birkenstock-shod yuppie-gone-guru natural healer, but … it's true. Nature is precisely balanced down to the atom.

Things come, things go. Hot and cold, night and day, rain and sun, bitter and sweet, democrats-republicans, life-death, high-low, good-not good, food in-food out, oceans-desserts, mountains-valleys, not too little-not too much, just enough of every extreme to strike a perfect balance.

Live in harmony and live well. Tinker with it too much or demand that the world conform to your preferences and you'll end up spinning out of control. I am not suggesting that we return to the Stone Age and spend our days picking berries and skinning hides. I am recommending, however, that we take responsibility for what we have created, both good and not so good, and evolve our thinking and our behavior to a level that can coexist with our natural, balanced state.

> *"Come and follow in our wake, you've not that much*
> *at stake. For we have plowed the seas, and smoothed*
> *the troubled waters.*
> *Come along, let's have some fun, seems our work is*
> *done. We'll barrel roll into the sun, just for starters."*
> — Jimmy Buffett, "Barometer Soup"

You know Jimmy Buffet? Probably you do, but you might not associate the Bard of Key West with moderation. Yet Buffet uses his music to describe what a proper perspective might look like. The lyrics of his songs can be fun, sarcastic, campy, and laced with wisdom, all at once. "Moderation," says the man who wrote "Wasted away again in Margaritaville", "seems to be the key," and he should know. He has gone to untold extremes during an unconventional rise to fame and fortune and, if you listen closely, he shares the wisdom of an experienced soul's quest for serenity, purpose, and internal symmetry. This-author-poet-pilot-father-sailor-balladeer ranks among the most successful entertainers of our time and is perhaps, the greatest sales-man the music industry has ever known. Don't call it luck. He achieved this insight by simply paying attention to the signals his instincts were sending—signals, I might add, that run consistently contrary to conventional wisdom about how to get ahead.

Getting ahead to Jimmy means being an original and a bit of an icono-clast. Jimmy does not play in concert halls, because he prefers to play at outdoor amphitheaters. Jimmy does not make videos. He produces musicals and writes best sellers. Jimmy does not cater to the press looking for free publicity. He mocks them. Jimmy barely gets radio time, yet he produces an album a year and they all sell well. Jimmy manages his career his own way rather than let others dictate his path to success.

The self-described "son of a son of a sailor" maintains an amazing schedule, manages a vast conglomerate, flies planes, sails boats, and writes songs, books, and musicals. His talent for maintaining personal balance and professional momentum should be an inspiration to us all.

Moderation, it turns out, is exactly what is required to maintain the kind of balanced approach needed to navigate successfully through our tan-gled web of pressing priorities. My tendency, and perhaps yours as well, is to dive into and dwell upon one major project or initiative at a time, ferociously work it to conclusion, take a breath, and move onto the next. Impatient and intense, my need for completion and closure of the current "mission" can be all consuming and frequently blinds me from other priorities (and opportunities) that deserve at least a modicum of attention.

It's as if I have an internal drill sergeant, barking commands and making demands. If I am painting our house, I will work from "dawn 'til dusk" until it's done. Mowing the lawn means the entire lawn, not just the back yard. Washing the car means inside and out; doing the taxes means completing every form; preparing a proposal means soup-to-nuts perfection ... and it means today. No compartmentalizer, I.

As a result, my thinking can become very linear rather than broad, expansive, or creative. I can feel overwhelmed if too much is pending and, as a result, most questions, requests, or demands from others are considered annoying and inappropriate. After all, can't they see that I'm busy?

> "... *The wrong thing is the right thing, until you lose control.*
> *I got this bank of bad habits in the corner of my soul* ...."
> — Jimmy Buffett, "Bank of Bad Habits"

But I changed. One day, a few years back, a chance glance in the mirror changed my perspective on this part of my life and eventually quieted my drill sergeant. I did not consciously instigate this self-study (I was just brushing my teeth), but it happened anyway, and I did not like what I saw. Staring back at me, of course, was me—only older, wrinkled, wider, hairier, and more run down than I had ever dared notice before. What in the hell happened here, I thought, and more importantly, what hasn't happened? Like a bolt of lightning, the answers came. What I had once considered to be some of my greatest qualities—determination, ambition, persistence, drive, and discipline—were now such a dominant part of my character that they were completely overwhelming my ability to balance them out with softer, equally important personality traits.

Like a once-sturdy table saw grown dull with overuse, I was prematurely wearing out and I knew that it was time to reevaluate and readjust my methods for managing conflicting priorities.

> "*There is no finer sensation in life than that which*
> *comes with victory over one's self* .... *Go forward*
> *to a goal of inward achievement, brushing aside*
> *all your old internal enemies as you advance.*"
> — Vash Young

Making full use of our partnership, I brought this revelation back to my semi-clairvoyant wife. She lectured willingly, I listened painfully, and what follows is a summary of what I learned.

There is more than one "You". There is the professional you, the spiritual you, the playful you, the parental you, the married you, the sibling you, the child you, and many more. All are in constant competition for your time, consideration, and support. The one in crisis will scream the loudest and demand the most attention while none of them are ever completely satisfied with the attention that they get. Each one of your "yous" is unique and has something wonderful to offer; however, only you can bring out their best. Balance and harmony depend on your ability to recognize and nurture the needs of the collective you, well in advance of a crisis or breakdown, so that you may capitalize on the joy that each one offers.

Do what you love. Remember, it was passion that kept Noah Webster going for 36 years before he completed his first dictionary. Same with Thomas Edison, who failed 10,000 times before creating the first incandescent lamp. It's much easier, however, if your passion loves you back. The greatest consequence of extreme behavior that is directed at a single priority in your life is that the other priorities begin to collaborate to make you miserable. Over-emphasize your professional life and watch your personal life go to hell before you can say "every other weekend and alternating holidays". It is often necessary to give preferential treatment to your personal and professional hot spots and it is probably impossible to equally attend to every desirable area. The trick to balanced activity is to invest your potential in measured doses rather than in screaming leaps, conserving enough to satisfy competing priorities in advance of any crisis. This can never be done perfectly, but it can be done much better if you plan and prioritize in advance.

Teach your children well. That's what Crosby, Stills, Nash and Young had in mind when they wrote the song of the same name. All children are our children; whether you conceived them or not is irrelevant. We must devote more time to their psychological development and to their emotional well-being rather than spend all of our time on their extracurricular "activities". They're our collaborative legacy and our mutual responsibility. In their memories we live eternally, in their hearts we are loved forever, and in their steps will come generations of practitioners of the traditions and principles that we have the opportunity to tutor them in today. They do have opinions of their own and a tendency not to listen very well, making the mentoring process occasionally … "difficult". However, the likelihood that the little folk will learn and practice all that we advocate improves dramatically when we spend the time to regularly reinforce our beliefs. Encourage and even mandate their participation in real discussions that build their confidence, establish priorities, promote critical thinking, and expand their world. Consistently practice what you preach, engage them, cherish them, be patient with them, and always include them. They are you, only smaller, more impressionable, and eager to learn.

Creating Your Priority Management Plan

So … what else to do? We know that it is time for a change. We recognize that it is time to go on the offensive. It is high time to stake your claim on each day and use what talents and tools you have been given to give your life meaning. You are worth every minute that you spend on making your life meaningful.

Put my money where my mouth is? Fair enough. The following is a priority management system that, when followed, will prove flexible enough to be realistic yet structured enough to ensure accountability and consistency. It will get you results.

Step One: Identify Your "Level I" High-Payoff Activities:

High-payoff activities are the things that we do or should be doing to advance us in the direction of the achievement of our objectives. When you completed your "Goal Planning Sheets" in the Section on Goal Setting in Chapter 3, you listed some of your high-payoff activities in the "Action Steps" section of each form. These are *Level I* activities that you determined would get you to where you want to be, both professionally and personally. Ideally, we would all make these Level I activities our highest priorities every minute of every day and, in so doing, maximize our ability to achieve our goals in the shortest time possible. If we had nothing else to do, and subsequently had no other conflicting priorities, this scenario would be the only prescription for success that we would ever need.

Realistically, however, we are constantly confronted with an over-whelming and ever-changing list of other priorities that interfere with, and often obliterate, our ability to stay focused on the things that matter the most. As the boundary between what we are doing and what we should be doing becomes blurred, it becomes increasingly difficult to distinguish which activities are worthy of our time and which are not. As a result, we tend to establish our priorities and build our "to-do lists" based on criteria that may not be relevant to the achievement of our objectives.

Here's a good example. At the beginning of each week I create an exhaus-tive to-do list that includes everything that must get done, things that should get done, and things that I would like to have done by the end of the week.

If I permit my instincts and preferences to establish my priorities, I will be drawn immediately to the activities that are easiest to dispense with, those that are late or have an imminent deadline, those that I'm afraid of not doing, those that I prefer to do, and those that I'm comfortable doing. While all of these activities may seem important, few of them, if any, qualify as true Level I activities.

> *"When our knowing exceeds our sensing, we*
> *will no longer be deceived by the illusions of our*
> *senses."*
>
> — Walter Russell

Level I activities are distinguishable from all other activities in the fol-lowing ways:

They are proactive rather than reactive. True "under the radar" operators, they will not "present" themselves to get done like an emergency or a crisis will. You must do something to make Level I activities happen. Unlike the uncontrollable, random, disruptive, and noisy characteristics that are typical of the fires that need to be put out, Level I activities are pre-planned and well organized. You have no choice but to deal with your personal and professional fires. Level I activities, however, require you to take the initiative and maintain it. Often, this needed drive is difficult to find because we are so caught up in reactive, pressure intensive, and deadline driven activities and events. Even when we do find it, this drive is difficult to maintain consistently due to interruptions, fatigue, and other "life" emergencies. Think about how often you have started and then stopped an exercise program or a special diet. Have you ever enthusiastically developed a new marketing program, a service, or prospecting system only to have it evaporate because there is never enough time to devote to the project? More good ideas and well-intended plans go down the drain for lack of follow-through than there are notes in a hymnal. The proactive nature of Level I activities makes them easy to put aside while we tend to something more urgent or more preferable. After only a few days, weeks, or months of neglect, they will no longer appear on the list of things to do at all. They will instead join the list of things we wish we had done.

They prevent a crisis rather than address a crisis. Larry Bird once said, "If you don't do your homework, you won't make your free throws." Translated from Bird-speak, that simply means to put the time in and do your homework. For instance, an unsolicited service call to an existing client may answer a risk management question that, left unanswered, might have grown into a service crisis. Take your exercise program, which keeps you healthy enough to avoid the heart attack that you otherwise might have had. Or how about regularly scheduled quality time spent with your children that helps prevent the broken family that might have resulted down the road? Rather than fight the daily fires, Level I activities tend to neutralize the arsonists so that the fires never occur. Because we never actually experience the crisis, it is often difficult to associate tangible results with the investment of the time and attention. The lack of concrete evidence that the Level I activity is "paying off" will often cause us to doubt the present-day value of our effort and chip away at our resolve. We find it easy to justify postponing these activities so that we may accommodate others that yield a more definitive or timely result. In short, we're not practicing our free throws.

They lack a sense of urgency. Level I activities are directed at long-term objectives that build or enhance your professional and personal life. Unlike the intense pressure that we feel when we are scrambling to finish an overdue project or responding to a client crisis, Level I activities lack "do or die" deadlines and rarely evoke short-term expectations for results from others. There is no immediate penalty for not executing a Level I activity on schedule. Many of us (me included), have a tendency to rank some of our priorities based upon the short-term, known consequences that we feel will result from not accomplishing the task rather than evaluating the overall contribution and worthiness of the activity. As a result, we will tend toward the activities that are pressing us the hardest and causing the highest degree of anxiety. Our quiet, less worrisome Level I activities become easy to ignore and put off for another day.

They do not provide instant gratification for your time and attention. Like a farmer patiently nurturing his crops, desired results are gradually achieved over a span of time, requiring consistent execution of planned activity. Progress is sometimes difficult to detect during each step in the plan and we must rely firmly on patience and self-discipline to stay focused and accountable. Generally, we must invest heavily in faith that reinforces the belief that in doing the right things, for the right reasons, with the right people, we will achieve the right result. In this age of instant access to anything, we have grown so accustomed to getting what we want when we want it, that our deliberate, gradual approach to lasting success conflicts with a pre-conditioned expectation of instant gratification. Staying true to your proactive, long-term plan almost always requires you to subdue the instincts that demand a speedy result while maintaining a consistent focus on the larger, long-term objective. This is not a wrestling match that we win easily.

Ironically, Level I activities are the most challenging to find time for, yet, when the time is found they yield the greatest returns. Once accomplished, your Level I activities leave you feeling exhilarated, more confident, directed, and formidable.

Clearly, these are the activities that matter the most, and it is our objective to spend more time engaged with them. The time that we need, however, must come from somewhere else, and this inherently means that we must spend less time involved with less productive, inferior activities. We will try to minimize the time spent with activities that are detrimental to our growth. We now know what we should be doing. It is now time, therefore, to decide what not to do.

"In the end we do battle only with ourselves. Once we understand this and focus our energy on what we can do to control our lives... we begin to gain important insights into how life works."
— H. Stanley Judd

Step Two: Categorize Your "Other" Activities:

Okay, we've covered proactive. Let's look at the reactive stuff. **Level II activities** are the reactive, in-the-moment responses to the urgent events that occur each day in our personal and professional lives. Lost car keys, downed computer servers, a sick child the day of your big client meeting— all are often unforeseen, unplanned, and uncontrollable; these are the crises, emergencies, surprises, and "fire drills" that create chaos, stress, fatigue, and frustration.

The list is endless—as are the headaches. Still, many Level II activities are unavoidable and uncontrollable; they happen and must be dealt with. Others, however, result from poorly executed Level I activities that could have eliminated or minimized the need to react. The claim dispute that you are forced to mediate between the carrier and the client could have been prevented altogether had a proactive risk management program been in place. The empty new business pipeline that the agency owner is badgering you about would still be flowing with opportunities if you had stuck to your channel marketing system. You would not be spending the weekend preparing a bid for a client who would not be bidding at all if your value-added service program had stayed in place.

These are just a few examples of common disruptions that could easily be avoided by staying consistently engaged in work related Level I activities. We could make a similar list for your personal disturbances; however, I think the point has been made.

You have enough real-life experience with Level II activities to know which are avoidable (therefore self-induced) and which are not. Although we can never completely eliminate Level II activities, we can definitely reduce the amount of time and composure that we lose to them by devoting consistent time to our Level I activities. We all inherently know this yet we all struggle with it. Why is this predicament so easy to identify yet so challenging to resolve?

> *"One might as well try to ride two horses moving in different directions, as to try to maintain in equal force two opposing or contradictory sets of desires."*
> — Robert Collier

It has become our nature to expect and desire instant and tangible rewards for our time and attention. Level II activities provide these rewards and give us a false sense of accomplishment. When we put out an administrative fire, manage a client crisis, or just beat the deadline for a proposal, we take a deep breath and see that we did something. Whether or not it could have been handled more efficiently or avoided altogether might be a secondary consideration; the fact is that we successfully dodged another bullet and we will live to see another day. The more bullets that we dodge, the better we get at it and the more conditioned we become to waiting for the gun to go off before we take action.

This romp can produce gallons of adrenaline and actually feel exhilarating. It also causes damaging levels of anxiety, stress, and emotional fatigue that eventually cause us to burn out. It is a popular way to live; however, it is not the good life.

Level III Activities are nefarious energy-drainers that can slow the most promising sales career. But if you like putting someone else's agenda ahead of your own, Level III Activities are for you. These are the "got-a-minute?" requests for your time from co-workers, impromptu phone calls just to chat, meetings that have nothing to do with what's important to you, and social commitments that string you out and hamper your effectiveness. These are the reports that you do that nobody really looks at, the little clients that demand large amounts of time, and the assigned projects that help others to achieve their objectives but do nothing for you. These are the countless "sacrificial" occasions when we put aside what is important to us in favor of what is important to somebody else. These are not worth your valuable time and here's why.

You're a team player, right? So it's only natural to give of yourself to help others and their causes. However, your giving becomes detrimental to you and to the recipient of your charity when your support is unconditional, unrestrained, and unrewarded. They become overly dependent upon your availability and you come to resent the time and attention that they need. You will eventually realize that you are unfairly taxing yourself and your agenda. You will drop hints the size of manhole covers and suggest that enough is enough and then marvel at their inability to recognize the inequity. Such shallowness, you thought, only exists in Hollywood or in Congress. So you might feel used, pestered, codependent, unappreciated, and taken advantage of by the clients, colleagues, friends, and family who live by the Latin term "Ubi Mea" (meaning, "where's mine?"). Eventually, when you are forced to come to terms with the imbalance, your frustration will lead to either an uncomfortable confrontation or a disheartening acceptance of the inconvenience. In either case, somebody usually gets hurt.

> *"Whatever the price, identify it now. What will*
> *you have to go through to get where you want to*
> *be?… There is a price you can pay to be free of the*
> *situation once and for all. It may be a fantastic*
> *price or a tiny one—but there is a price."*
> — Harry Browne

Effectively managing Level III activities means managing the expectations that others have regarding your availability and willingness to assist them. Some of these intrusions are unavoidable they come with the job or they are a part of life. Many of them, however, can and should be prevented or at least deferred by proactively establishing, communicating, and consistently maintaining reasonable boundaries. Most people will respect your limitations if they understand that you have them. However, nobody can be expected to correctly assume what they are and to know when they are in place. Simple techniques such as using your voice mail to screen your calls, closing your office door when you do not wish to be interrupted, sharing your calendar, and pre-scheduling what would otherwise be drop-in visits will make you accessible without being openly available. These countermeasures are absolutely appropriate and necessary. Regardless of the length of each interruption, each time that we are interrupted we lose our momentum and our concentration. It can be extremely difficult to regain this lost ground and get back on track. Experience the dreaded double interruption (those occasions when the initial interruption is interrupted by a second one), and it can be all day before you are able to circle back to the original project. We must learn to hold our ground.

Other activities that qualify under Level III are those things that could be done by others that we elect to do ourselves. The things that we can delegate but choose not to because we enjoy the activity or we might be bashful about intruding on another's time. Perhaps we are concerned that it won't be done right, or it won't be done on time, or we think that it's quicker just to do it ourselves. Perhaps so initially, but things never taught are things never learned and things never learned by others are forever ours to do, until we teach them.

Level IV Activities are the out-and-out time wasters that contribute nothing in support of the achievement of our objectives and, in many cases, prove detrimental to our growth. These are our escape behaviors, the things that we do to retreat from the pressure and fatigue of Level II or to get away from the emotional tug-of-war associated with Level III. Simply stated, Level IV activities enable us to tune-out reality and take a conscious vacation from our lives and our feelings. Often confused with Level I "recreational" activities or thought to contain some entertainment value, these behaviors differ in that they lack productive intention and they are often practiced to an extreme. For example, taking a quick nap is a Level I act, sleeping away the day is Level IV. A fun night out with friends—Level I, a weekend binge—Level IV. Watching a favorite TV show—Level I, watching anything that is on all night, Level IV. While the desired effect may be to deaden emotions and have some quiet time, the physical and psychological consequences of habitual indulgence in Level IV escape can be significant and damaging. These include lethargy, boredom, depression, and isolation—the cornerstones for addiction to alcohol, drugs, and overeating.

> "If we triumph in the little things of our common
> hour, we are sure to triumph in our lives."
> — unknown

It is not my intention to be an alarmist or a purist; we all have our escape activity and we are all entitled to our downtime. Most of us will never be endangered by it. My goal is to help you to identify what you do, why you do it, and the effect it has on your ability to manage your objectives. The fact is that we can find the relief and relaxation that we are seeking in our Level IV activities in many of our Level I activities if we simply look there first before falling into the Level IV trap or habit. In fact, at this very moment I am weary of writing and I am in the process of making a Level I vs. Level IV decision.

I can throw on my shoes and go for a run or I can flip my computer screen over and play a few games of Solitaire. The run will clear my mind, relieve stress, and keep me on track to achieve my fitness goal. The game will clear my mind and contribute nothing. As appealing as the Level IV choice may seem, I know that I'll feel better at the end of the day if I choose the run so … today I'm tying up my shoes and heading out the door. Tomorrow, who knows, but at least I'll be aware of my options and their impact.

> *"Happiness does not come from doing easy work*
> *but from the afterglow of satisfaction that comes*
> *after the achievement of a difficult task that*
> *demanded our best."*
> — Theodore I. Rubin

The greatest difference between our high-payoff activities and all of the other things that we do each day is that high-payoff activities are proactive and productive. When you are consistently engaged in these personal and professional activities at the high-payoff level, you establish a balance and rhythm to your day. You live with a sense of purpose and feel more in control because you are under control. Unavoidable interruptions and unforeseeable intrusions on your schedule cause less friction than they otherwise would because your perspective is different. You are able to filter out much of the noise and manage your way through most calamities with a heightened level of indifference. Your method for establishing priorities becomes more analytical than emotional and any tendency to plunge directly into the next reactive task gets restrained. Directed by your internal compass, you move through your day paying attention to your surroundings and reacting when necessary, but you do so without ever losing sight of the horizon.

You, my friend, become very smooth and very cool.

On the following page is a chart that will help you to qualify and categorize your activities. I keep a copy of this chart on my desk and in my planner to help me get my head straight before I set my priorities.

Activity Identifiers

Level I
<u>Activities:</u> High-payoff, preventative deliberate steps toward an established objective. Enhancing and enriching. Generally scheduled and controllable. <u>Characteristics:</u> Pre-planned, proactive activities that yield gradual or intangible return. Reduce crisis and provide a strong sense of freedom and accomplishment. <u>Emotional Effect:</u> Confidence building, energizing, exhilarating, motivating, calming, and relieving.

Level II
<u>Activities:</u> Crisis driven, emergencies, missed deadlines, fires, etc. Damaging and unproductive. Generally uncontrolled, random, and haphazard. <u>Characteristics:</u> Unplanned, reactive activities that yield instant results for the time and attention. Provides adrenaline rush and false sense of accomplishment. Confusing and exhausting. <u>Emotional Effect:</u> Anxiety, negative stress, fatigue, depression, anger, and frustration.

Level III
Activities: Interruptions, others' priorities, favors, unproductive meetings, etc. Things that could be delegated but are not. <u>Characteristics:</u> Unplanned, reactive activities that yield no return. Pressing issues for others that have little or no effect on you. <u>Emotional Effect:</u> Anger, frustration, annoyance, co-dependence, and resentments.

Level IV
<u>Activities:</u> Escape-like behavior used to avoid or distract. Desensitized, solitary, and non-productive. Generally controlled and deliberate. <u>Characteristics:</u> Planned, habit-forming activities that yield no return. Provide relief from stress and deaden the emotions. <u>Emotional Effect:</u> Depression, lethargy, boredom, loneliness, isolation, and addictions.

Once the activity is categorized in this way, it is much easier to develop a priority management plan that uses logic rather than emotions, personal preferences, or environmental pressures to determine what to do, how much of it to do, and in what order to do it. For instance, if you have an established production objective for the coming year that represents a 30% increase over your current level of production, you know that you will need to spend 30% more time engaged in the high-payoff activities that will generate the sales—the activities that are categorized as Level I. More production means more time devoted to producing.

Rather than extending your workday by 30% and run the risk of interfering with some of your personal objectives, it is more practical to find the time within the confines of your current workday. This inherently means that some things will have to go and less time will be spent on other, less productive activities. In this instance, I would normally suggest reallocating 10% of the time that you spend in each of the other three levels (II, III, & IV) into Level I so that you may accommodate the increase in high-payoff activity. Having categorized your activity as we described, it should be relatively easy to find and eliminate the inferior activity and create the "space" required in Level I. On the other hand, finding these efficiencies and making the appropriate adjustments would be extremely difficult without defining the value of the activities. This kind of approach does not require a radical restructuring of your work habits and routines; it merely calls for some reasonable adjustments and some forethought.

> *"Concentrate; put all your eggs in one basket and watch that basket ...."*
>
> — Andrew Carnegie

Step Three: Building Your Weekly Activity Menu

Earlier in this chapter I mentioned that I start each week with a comprehensive to-do list that itemizes *everything* that I can think of that must get done, should get done, and that I want to have done by the end of the week. Experience has taught me that this step is a crucial one and the more thorough I am here, the better off I am during the week. Please remember, however, that the list is a simmering one—as the week rolls out you'll be adding unforeseen or forgotten items to your "activity menu". The objective is a good start, not a complete forecast.

Starting this Sunday, allow an hour or so to take a good look at your week ahead. Make a list of everything you hope to accomplish, both personally and professionally, regardless of how trivial the activities may seem. Be sure to include all of the activities that you have listed on your goal sheets and especially remember to include activities for you and you alone. Things like reading, exercising, shopping, fishing, dancing, painting, etc. This is the stuff that rarely makes any list.

Also include time for your mate, time to find one if you are without, and time for your children. List activities that you used to do, but no longer do (activities that you personally enjoyed or found to be professionally effective), things that you presently do but do not do often enough and especially, include those things that you always wanted to do but have yet to find the time, or the money, or the energy, or the … whatever.

The first few times that you do this, you might struggle and perhaps feel overwhelmed. Your list of activities will be a long one and it will become quickly apparent that you cannot possibly do everything that shows up on the list. Do not be discouraged; this is not a checklist designed for the purpose of knocking things off. Rather, it is a menu of available options intended to help you see, select, and schedule the most productive activity. Treat it like a menu that you would find at any restaurant. The objective of the menu is to provide you with a complete listing of the available offerings. There, you would not even consider ordering every item that appears but would instead make a selection based upon appeal, appetite, or diet. Your activity will be selected from your "menu" based upon the degree of contribution to the achievement of your objectives.

Step Four: Establishing Your Weekly Priorities

Once the list is complete, review it and pick out those activities that will most effectively move you in the direction of the achievement of your personal and professional objectives. Almost without exception, these will be Level I, high-payoff activities. As a reminder, most of these activities are proactive, will not seem urgent, and will have no immediate result attached to them. Because these activities are not screaming for immediate attention, they are the ones most often ignored or displaced by life's distractions. These are the many things we promise ourselves we will get to, eventually, someday.

Next, identify the Level II activities on your list, the Level III activities, and the Level IV activities. In the beginning, it is quite common to have more Level II activities than all of the others combined. This is a clear indicator of just how reactive most of our activity is and how much time we actually devote to responding to urgencies and emergencies—doing things that repair but never build.

I am not suggesting that we ignore or delay action on any of the Level II items. To do so would be irresponsible and the consequences extreme. I am suggesting that we give equal credibility to the Level I activities that will inevitably minimize the need to spend so much time on the Level II stuff. The same holds true for the Level III and Level IV activities. We shouldn't become so rigidly disciplined that we don't leave some room for others and we will never become so orderly that Level IV will completely disappear. We are only aiming for improved coordination and regulation, not complete elimination.

> *"In the last analysis, the individual person is responsible for living his own life and for 'finding himself'. If he persists in shifting his responsibility to somebody else, he fails to find out the meaning of his own existence."*
>
> — Thomas Merton

On the following page you will find a sample of a partial activity menu (a real list would be much longer than this one) that has been rated by Levels. On the page after that one, I have included a sample call list that I fill out while developing the activity menu. I use a manual sheet; others prefer to use contact management software or something similar. Regardless of the format, filling out a call sheet with the names and numbers of your contacts in advance of making the calls will allow you to make your calls in blocks without having to waste time looking for numbers. It also enables you to be completely portable and works well in the car. Like the activity menu, it is variable—I add to it and delete from it throughout each day.

WEEKLY ACTIVITY MENU

FOR THE WEEK ENDING 9/30/03

Professional Activity	Frequency	Tier	Personal Activity	Frequency	Tier
Clear E-mail Backlog	28	II	Run 3.5 miles	5 Days	I
Finish pipeline report	1	II	Neighbor's Cookout	1	II
Attend Agency Picnic	1	II	Take Daughter to Dance	1	I
XYZ Corp Sales Call	1	I	Wash the Cars	1	II
Prep for XYZ Corp Call	1	II	Review Kids Homework	5 Days	I
Return Calls*	3	I	Watch Monday Night FB	1	I
Return Calls*	7	II	Return Calls*	4	II
Return Calls*	14	III	Pay Bills	1	II
Make Referral Request*	2	I	Repair Shower	1	II
Finish ABC Co. Renewal	1	II	Watch TV	6 Days	IV
Make New Bus. Calls*	10	I	Be Home for Dinner	3	I
Investigate LMN Co Claim	1	II	Next Flying Lessons	2	I
Send E-Clipping File	50	I	Son's Soccer Game	1	I
Make Service Calls*	5	I	Writing Workshop	1	I
Pre-approach Letters*	10	I	Refrig. Light Bulb	1	II
Lunch with DEF	1	I	Get New CDs	5	I
Attend Service Meeting	1	II	Lights out by 11:00 P.M.	5	I
Complete Carrier Survey	1	II	Breakfast Each Morning	Daily	I
Finish QRS Proposal	1	II	Study for Flight Exam	4	I
Online Industry News	Daily	I	Review Stocks Online	5	I
DEF Claims Review	1	II	Send Dad, Sister e-mail	2	II
Create Football Pool	1	IV	Mow the Lawn	2	II

* Use supplemental call sheet to list names and telephone numbers

WEEKLY CALL SHEET

FOR THE WEEK ENDING 9/30/03

PROSPECT CALLS		REFERRAL CALLS		SERVICE CALLS	
Name, Company	Phone #, ext.	Name, Company	Phone #, ext.	Name, Company	Phone #, ext.
Name, Company	Phone #, ext.	Name, Company	Phone #, ext.	Name, Company	Phone #, ext.
Name, Company	Phone #, ext.	Name, Company	Phone #, ext.	Name, Company	Phone #, ext.
Name, Company	Phone #, ext.	Name, Company	Phone #, ext.	Name, Company	Phone #, ext.
Name, Company	Phone #, ext.	Name, Company	Phone #, ext.	Name, Company	Phone #, ext.
Name, Company	Phone #, ext.	Name, Company	Phone #, ext.	Name, Company	Phone #, ext.
Name, Company	Phone #, ext.	Name, Company	Phone #, ext.	Name, Company	Phone #, ext.
Name, Company	Phone #, ext.	Name, Company	Phone #, ext.	Name, Company	Phone #, ext.
Name, Company	Phone #, ext.	Name, Company	Phone #, ext.	Name, Company	Phone #, ext.
Name, Company	Phone #, ext.	Name, Company	Phone #, ext.	Name, Company	Phone #, ext.

RETURN CALLS		PERSONAL CALLS		E-MAILS	
Name, Company	Phone #, ext.	Name, Company	Phone #, ext.	Name	e-mail
Name, Company	Phone #, ext.	Name, Company	Phone #, ext.	Name	e-mail
Name, Company	Phone #, ext.	Name, Company	Phone #, ext.	Name	e-mail
Name, Company	Phone #, ext.	Name, Company	Phone #, ext.	Name	e-mail
Name, Company	Phone #, ext.	Name, Company	Phone #, ext.	Name	e-mail
Name, Company	Phone #, ext.	Name, Company	Phone #, ext.	Name	e-mail
Name, Company	Phone #, ext.	Name, Company	Phone #, ext.	Name	e-mail
Name, Company	Phone #, ext.	Name, Company	Phone #, ext.	Name	e-mail
Name, Company	Phone #, ext.	Name, Company	Phone #, ext.	Name	e-mail
Name, Company	Phone #, ext.	Name, Company	Phone #, ext.	Name	e-mail

Step Five: Identify Opportunity Costs

Opportunity costs are the penalties we pay for choosing one activity over another and/or the cost of inefficiency. What we do and how we do it is too often a function of past practice and current habits which limit our ability to identify an alternative course of action. Keep a close eye out for activities that you presently do that could be done better or more efficiently by somebody else. For example, I used to spend a day per weekend mowing my lawn. When I added up the true cost involved with doing it myself—costs that included the value of my time, the gas, the oil, the maintenance of the equipment, etc.—I realized that I could pay for a professional service and actually save money. Not only that, they also do a better job. The same is true for most of my large projects around the house. The fact that I'm capable of repairing or building almost anything that we need doesn't mean that I will save money by doing it myself. In most cases, I actually come out behind.

Another example—I travel frequently and for years I would almost always drive myself to the airport and pay for parking. The trip to the airport takes about an hour and a half and I would allow another hour to park, check-in, and find the gate. A friend suggested that I look into a car service and, after comparing the fee against the true cost of driving myself, I realized that although the rate was more expensive than the parking, I could work in the car and leave for the airport a full 45 minutes later than I otherwise would. Still other examples include working on small accounts rather than large ones, writing letters rather than sending e-mails, having lunch with an associate rather than a client, and so on.

Once the value of your time is correctly calculated into the priority management process, you will immediately be able to identify the activities that yield the greatest return for your time and attention. Here is a chart that will help you calculate the value of your time. As you review your activity menu, evaluate what you plan to do and how you plan to do it while asking yourself the following question: "Is what I am going to do worth the time I'm going to spend doing it?"

> *"Today, knowledge has power. It controls access to opportunity and advancement."*
>
> — Peter F. Drucker

How much does time cost you each day?

The next chart shows the value of your time, by the hour and by the minute, based on your annual income, working 240 eight-hour days per year. This assumes a five-day workweek adjusted for normal vacation time and holidays.

Your Annual Income Is:	Each Hour You Spend:	Each Minute You Spend:
$25,000	13.02	.22
30,000	15.62	.26
35,000	18.23	.30
40,000	20.83	.35
45,000	23.44	.39
50,000	26.04	.43
60,000	31.25	.52
70,000	36.46	.61
80,000	41.67	.69
90,000	46.88	.78
100,000	52.08	.87
125,000	65.10	1.09
150,000	78.13	1.30
175,000	91.15	1.52
200,000	104.17	1.74
250,000	130.21	2.17
300,000	156.25	2.60
400,000	208.33	3.47
500,000	260.42	4.34
1,000,000	520.83	8.68

Revisiting the sample activity menu that we used in Step 4, we can see how some of the activity was re-categorized into other levels based upon our opportunity cost analysis.

On the professional list:

- Some of the e-mail responses were moved to Tier III because they contributed little.
- The agency picnic was considered nice, politically correct, but not needed.
- Somebody else can handle the claims investigation for a small client.
- The lunch with DEF, another producer, is more social than helpful.
- Attending the Service Department meeting is usually non-productive.
- Completing the carrier survey may help them but does little for me.

On the personal list:

- The neighbor's cookout is really for the kids.
- Washing the cars by hand takes too long; the car wash is better.
- Monday Night Football is not showing a favorite team—why bother.
- Mowing the lawn could be done with a service or one of the kids.

The point to remember is that there are always alternative solutions to getting things done. When reviewing your options remain as intellectual and analytical as possible. Pretend to be an unbiased advisor to your own schedule. Even if you choose to do things the same way that you always have, you at least know that you are making a choice that you can rationalize.

REVISED WEEKLY ACTIVITY MENU

FOR THE WEEK ENDING 9/30/03

Professional Activity	Frequency	Tier	Personal Activity	Frequency	Tier
Clear E-mail Backlog	28	II, III	Run 3.5 miles	5 Days	I
Finish pipeline report	1	II	Neighbor's Cookout	1	III
Attend Agency Picnic	1	III	Take Daughter to Dance	1	I
XYZ Corp Sales Call	1	I	Wash the Cars	1	IV
Prep for XYZ Corp Call	1	II	Review Kids Homework	5 Days	I
Return Calls*	3	I	Watch Monday Night FB	1	IV
Return Calls*	7	II	Return Calls*	4	II
Return Calls*	14	III	Pay Bills	1	II
Make Referral Request*	2	I	Repair Shower	1	II
Finish ABC Co. Renewal	1	II	Watch TV	6 Days	IV
Make New Bus. Calls*	10	I	Be Home for Dinner	3	II
Investigate LMN Claim	1	IV	Next Flying Lessons	2	I
Send E-Clipping File	50	I	Son's Soccer Game	1	I
Make Service Calls*	5	I	Writing Workshop	1	I
Pre-approach Letters*	10	I	Refrig. Light Bulb	1	II
Lunch with DEF	1	III	Get New CDs	5	I
Attend Service Meeting	1	III	Lights out by 11:00 P.M.	5	I
Complete Carrier Survey	1	IV	Breakfast Each Morning	Daily	I
Finish QRS Proposal	1	II	Study for Flight Exam	4	I
Online Industry News	Daily	I	Review Stocks Online	5	I
DEF Claims Review	1	II	Send Dad, Sister E-mail	2	II
Create Football Pool	1	IV	Mow the Lawn	2	IV

Step Six: Building A Weekly Calendar

Having scrutinized our activities, categorized them by Level, and created a weekly call sheet, we now know what we want to do and to whom we want to do it. All that remains to be done is the construction of a schedule that will tell us when the activities can be accomplished. Prior to developing our schedule for the week, it is important for us to take a step back and remind ourselves of a few qualifying factors, namely:

- **The schedule is not fixed.** Even the most precise plans change as unpredictable circumstances intrude. Rather than fight this fact of life, we are going to build a calendar that is flexible enough to tolerate changes without sending us into a tailspin. Remember that a professional football team spends months preparing a game plan for an opponent only to have it change the minute the game begins. Rather than abandon the original plan, the coaching staff and players make continual adjustments that improve their chances for a successful outcome. We too will need to adjust.

- **What gets done is more important than when it gets done.** Unlike many time management systems, our focus is on the day and the week, not on the minutes. We will not accomplish every task in the time that we estimate that it will take nor will we start every initiative on time. Our goal is to end the week with most of our scheduled activities completed.

- **You've got rhythm!** Some of us are morning people and some of us are night owls. Throughout the day we experience periods of time when our energy level is high and our ability to focus improves, followed by lulls in both. Add to this our normal mood swings that can vary from highly motivated to melancholy and we can have a frustrating experience if we try to schedule high-performance tasks into blocks of time when we would rather do nothing at all. Conversely, we do not want to waste our peak production hours on trivial tasks. Once you are aware of your own rhythms, you will find them to be fairly consistent and you can plan accordingly. I get grumpy and become easily distracted if I go without eating for too long so ... I have little snacks throughout the day to keep me sharp. Also, don't try to mimic someone else. In an attempt to impress or fit in, too many night people struggle to behave like morning people and visa-versa. Respect yourself and your natural cycles.

- **Pay attention to your attention span!** Even when you are operating during peak performance time, the longer you stay engrossed in one task the more difficult it becomes and the more energy it takes to pay attention to what you are doing. Most attention spans range between 30-90 minutes after which time you hit a wall and begin to require more and more energy to stay focused. Keep working and you will soon be depleted. Know what your attention span is and don't fight it. Take little breaks at appropriate times—get a cup of coffee, a drink of water, check your voice mail, or take a walk around the office to stretch. Then get back to it and see how refreshed you feel.

- **Be real.** You will not complete everything on your list. In fact, you may even add more activity than you dispense with as the week rolls out. Even if by some miracle all that you had to do was Tier I activities, you would still have to make some tough decisions about what gets done and what doesn't. You will always be dealing with a never-ending list of competing priorities; flexibility and practicality are called for.

With these conditions in place, we are ready to develop the calendar. You will need to use a weekly calendar that is formatted like the one shown on the next page.

	Mon	Tues	Wed	Thurs	Fri	Sat	Sun
7:00-8:00							
8:00-9:00							
9:00-10:00							
10:00-11:00							
11:00-12:00							
12:00-1:00							
1:00-2:00							
2:00-3:00							
3:00-4:00							
4:00-5:00							
5:00-6:00							
6:00-7:00							
7:00-8:00							
8:00-9:00							
9:00-10:00							
10:00-11:00							

I suggest that you use a web-enabled calendar and activity planner that can be accessed from the office as well as at home and on the road. If you have a laptop, you can also use any one of a number of contact manager/ activity planner software products that are available (the most popular ones are Outlook, ACT, Goldmine, and Maximizer). At the very least, use a manual calendar that opens to display an entire week.

With the activity menu and call sheet in front of us, we are going to select a limited number of Level I activities and schedule them into the week ahead. Knowing full well that you will not be able to commit to every Level I activity that you have recorded, let alone every activity on the menu, it would be counter-productive to fill up every time-slot on the calendar without any hope of getting it all done. Although it might be aesthetically pleasing, the calendar would be too jammed up to be workable.

It is also important to remember that life is far too unpredictable to schedule everything precisely and, to avoid frustration or failure, we accept this reality rather than trying to fight it. I suggest that you begin by scheduling only 2-3 professional Tier I activities per day and 2-3 personal Tier I activities per day in these first few weeks. If you find yourself completing these assignments with ease, you can add more. Conversely, if you struggle, you can limit yourself even further.

The goal is to develop a consistent and determined commitment to these high- payoff activities at a pace that is practical and manageable. Your priority management system is designed to get you to your objectives over time, not overnight.

So ... here we go:

Starting with Monday, select your first Level I activity, estimate the time that it will take to accomplish the task, and box out the time on your calendar. Keep in mind that **first thing in the morning may not be the best time to schedule your first Level I activity.** Many of us (non-morning people) need time in the morning to set-up the day, meet with the staff, return a few calls, etc. If you are in the habit of taking this morning time to settle in, continue to take it (I usually schedule my first Level I for 9:00 a.m.)

	Monday	**Tuesday**
7:00-8:00		
8:00-9:00		
9:00-10:00	Make 5 Customer Service calls	
10:00-11:00		

According to the example shown above, at 9:00 a.m. on Monday, my door will close, my call sheet will come out, and I'll start smiling and dialing. I will not permit interruptions, I will not answer my phone when it rings, and I will not settle for anything other than completing the assignment. At this point, I don't really know how long it will take. If everybody that I'm calling is in—I could exceed the hour that I have estimated. If I get only voice mail greetings—I'll be done in 15 minutes. Either way, I'm only going to focus on the activity I can control—making the dials—the rest is out of my hands. The objective is the dials, not the conversation. In fact, I don't mind leaving proactive customer service messages on voicemail one bit. The positive client touch is made, the impact is effective, and I finish early. Advantage ... me.

I often make my Tier III calls and many of my "quick-answers-to-questions" Tier II calls during lunch or after hours with every intention of getting voice mail and avoiding an unnecessary conversation. I never return Tier IV calls.

Schedule your next Level I activity for sometime later in the morning or early afternoon. Try to schedule your high-payoff time each day by leaving large blocks of time in between other activities that will act as buffer zones and allow for flexibility. This way, we leave plenty of time to accommodate all of the normal daily activity and, in the event that we do run late with our first Level I, we are not bumping right into another high-payoff time slot. The trick is to chip away at the truly meaningful stuff throughout the day while fencing with all of the other impositions on your time.

	Monday	**Tuesday**
7:00-8:00		
8:00-9:00		
9:00-10:00	Make 5 Customer Service calls	
10:00-11:00		
11:00-12:00		
12:00-1:00		
1:00-2:00	Send Pre-Approach Letters (10)	
2:00-3:00		

Finish scheduling the remainder of the week in the same manner. Do not put your other activities on the calendar at all, keep them on your activity menu and complete them as time permits and within the buffer zones that exist between the high-payoff activities. Your completed calendar will look similar to this:

	Monday	Tuesday	Wednes-day	Thursday	Friday	Saturday	Sunday
7:00-8:00	Breakfast	Breakfast	Breakfast	Breakfast	Breakfast		
8:00-9:00						Breakfast	
9:00-10:00	Make 5 Customer Service calls	Return Calls		Send E-Clipping File (50)		Soccer	Breakfast
10:00-11:00			XYZ Corp Sales Call		Return Calls	Soccer	
11:00-12:00			XYZ Corp Sales Call				Flight Lesson
12:00-1:00			XYZ Corp Sales Call				
1:00-2:00	Send Pre-Approach Letters (10)		XYZ Corp Sales Call	Check on-line news, Review Stocks		Run	
2:00-3:00		New Business Calls (5)			New Business Calls (5)	Study for Flight Exam	Run
3:00-4:00							
4:00-5:00	Check on-line news, Review Stocks		Referral Requests (2)			Flight Lesson	
5:00-6:00		Run			Run		
6:00-7:00			Check on-line news, Review Stocks	Run		Father/Daughter Dance	Review Homework
7:00-8:00	Dinner			Dinner	Dinner	Father/Daughter Dance	
8:00-9:00	Review Homework		Review Homework		Check on-line news, Review Stocks	Father/Daughter Dance	
9:00-10:00		Check on-line news, Review Stocks		Review Homework		Father/Daughter Dance	
10:00-11:00	Study for Flight Exam		Study for Flight Exam		Study for Flight Exam		

You have completed your calendar and you now have a reasonable prediction of how the coming week is going to shape up. You have proactively established your priorities to avoid having to make crucial time management decisions in the heat of the moment when you are most likely to be impulsive and reactive. This is the reason why we create the menu, call sheet, and calendar on Sunday.

By Monday, or at any other time during the week, we are already fully engaged and will find it too difficult to withdraw, reflect, and reorganize our perspective and our priorities. A proactive hour on Sunday is the catalyst for an effective and efficient week.

Still, your weekly calendar is only your trail map for the week. It is your game plan that will be adjusted and revised many times as events unfold. The only thing that we can predict with absolute certainty is that unpredictable events will occur and upset our preconceived plan for the week. Be ready to move your Level I activities up and back and from side to side. Work your calendar like a game of chess—strategically and logically. If you keep it in front of you and follow it with determination, focusing on what gets done while being flexible with when, you will feel a great sense of satisfaction by week's end. As weeks turn into months and months into years, you will realize that in spite of all that did not get done, what did get done made a difference.

Additional priority management tips to help you during the week:

Get clean and stay clean.

Every now and again I bump into somebody that tries to convince me that a cluttered office is a sign of a real worker. They often go on to say that a clean desk signifies that the person doesn't have enough to do. Ah, no. If you wish to stay mentally organized then you must also be physically organized. I have heard all of the alibis and justifications for maintaining a sloppy work area—"I know where everything is," "I'm afraid I'll forget it," "I'm afraid that I'll lose it," and the ever popular "I'll clean it up tomorrow".

Don't buy any of them.

It is much more difficult to stay focused on what you are doing when you are surrounded by reminders of other things that need doing as well. Consciously, you may think that you are paying attention to what you are working on, but subconsciously, your "mind's eye" is constantly scanning your work environment and keeping track of everything else that it sees and hears. Unable to prioritize on its own, your subconscious will flood you with reminders, worries, concerns, and doubts about what you are and are not doing. All of this noise interferes with your ability to concentrate.

So ... clean your office and your work area. Move your "in-box" out of sight to keep it out of mind. An in-box on your desk is an invitation for people to interrupt you while they put stuff in it. File your piles and toss the stuff that you been meaning to read but haven't gotten to yet if it is more than a week or two old. If you must keep certain pending files out—keep them behind you and out of scanning range. Turn your "e-mail notifier" function off so that you are not interrupted every time you get a new e-mail. It is better to scan your e-mail and your voice mail when you decide to. Keep your desktop as vacant as possible—reserving your workspace for work in progress. The fewer the distractions, the easier it is to focus. And, *no music.* Background noise of any kind, pleasant as it may sound, is nothing short of disruptive to your ability to concentrate. Be clean and be quiet.

Schedule your appointments in clusters, months in advance.

The more proactive you are with your schedule, the easier it is to control your time. Because you initiate Level I appointments, you can schedule them well in advance and you can group them together by geographic proximity to avoid excessive or redundant travel. When you call to schedule these appointments, your client or prospect instantly recognizes you as a person who is busy, patient, and well-organized. They will appreciate the proactive nature of your call and their availability to meet with you is dramatically increased because they are usually not scheduled that far in advance. In the event that they are busy, be prepared to offer an alternative date when you plan to be in the area that is even further out. This again sends the right message and helps you to stay in control of your strategy.

When we leave it up to the client or prospect to pick the appointment date and time or we try to schedule our appointments in the current week, we sound too available, too unorganized, and sometimes too desperate. A proactive appointment is as good next month as it is today so ... think and plan ahead. Now on Sunday when we sit down to build our weekly calendar, we can schedule our activity around our appointments rather than trying to squeeze our appointments into the midst of our activity.

Two final suggestions on appointments. If your position requires you to schedule four appointments per week or more, pre-select consistent days in the week that will be your "appointment" days. For instance, I try to fit all of my new business and service calls into either Tuesday or Thursday. As the week begins, I use Monday to prepare for my Tuesday calls, Wednesday to follow up from Tuesday and to prepare for Thursday, and Friday to follow up from Thursday. On my appointment days, I start from home and end at home and never go near the office. This allows me to focus entirely on the clients and prospects without distraction.

Finally, I suggest that you create adequate buffer zones between each scheduled appointment. Allocate enough time to permit each appointment to run long and to get to and prepare for the next call without being rushed. There is nothing worse than arriving late, leaving early, and being unprepared for a client or prospect. If you do not need the time, use it to return calls, get the car washed, etc.

Make productive use of your time in the car.

Just because you are on the road doesn't mean you can't be knocking items off your "to do" list. In fact, the least productive place for me to be is in a chair behind a desk. The opportunity that I'm looking for is most always found outside of my office and meeting rooms; rarely does it find me at my desk. For that reason, I remain perfectly portable. I return most of my phone calls from the car, carry my laptop wherever I go, and keep all vital information with me in my brief case. I can work from anywhere and I can work at any time. The time I spend in the car used to be time wasted. I'd plop down in the seat, start it up, turn on the radio, and spend the trip complaining about traffic while semi-listening to whatever was playing.

I often thought of it as downtime—productive time to spend alone with my thoughts. Then I realized that I wasn't thinking of anything productive and I decided to change. Now, I return most of my calls from the car, listen to books on tape, and check in with the news and the market. This change in behavior converted Level IV time into usable time. Get portable, do the same, and be extra careful with the cell phone while driving.

Get off the phone.

It's good to be cyber-savvy. Use your e-mail as often as possible and train your clients and colleagues to do the same. Using e-mail permits you to organize your thoughts, communicate efficiently and effectively, and provides you with an electronic record of all correspondence.

Rather than fax, you can attach all pertinent documentation and you can consolidate all of your client information into an electronic file. Reduce the paper; reduce the time spent shuffling paper. Reduce the time spent on the phone, reduce the time spent sorting through messages and chasing down information. So, get e-smart.

Managing the System

There are only a few things that are mandatory for the participants in our training programs because I prefer to have each participant select what to use and what not to use from the available options. This priority management system, however, is a requirement for everybody. Of course, there is plenty of room for interpretation and customization according to the needs of each person in the program; however, non-compliance with the concept is not acceptable.

My demands for adhering to the process are justified. Having worked with thousands of you over the years, I can say with complete confidence that those who do this part of the program well, do well, and those that don't follow these guidelines do not do well. It is the foundation that supports the entire process.

If you work this simple little exercise into a habit and stay with it for a few months, you will feel better and accomplish more than ever before. If you do not in fact feel better, I will refund the price you paid for this book and you may return to your old system with my blessing.

This priority management system was not picked up from anything read or discovered in a classroom. It is the product of countless experiments with time management systems that never proved appropriate or effective in real life. It is the result of trial and error, of learning on-the-job what really works and what does not. It is the finished product that can only come from an honest self-evaluation.

When I finally gave up the need to have absolute control of time and gave in to the natural order of the world around me, I discovered an instinctive tempo to follow; a cadence that keeps me in step with the way life should unfold. I am still not capable of planning with enough perfection to fulfill every wish, but I am wise enough now to embrace imperfection and to work with it.

You, too, will hear your own drummer as time goes by, and will develop a cadence that is natural for you. As you make progress toward your objectives, you will realize, as I did, that personal and professional success in life has much less to do with luck and intellect than you thought. You will see that the right combination of determination, discipline, honesty, flexibility, creativity, and hard work will take you anywhere you wish to go and permit you to convert your wildest dreams into reality.

Here again are the steps in our process in a quick reference outline:

The Priority Management System

Step 1 – Identify Level I Activities

- Proactive
- Preventive
- Not urgent
- No instant results

Step 2 – Categorize Other Activities

- Level II – urgent and reactive
- Level III – other's priorities
- Level IV – time wasters

Step 3 – Build A Weekly Activity Menu

- Start on Sunday
- List all potential personal activities
- List all potential professional activities
- Create a Supplemental Call Sheet

Step 4 – Establish Priorities

- Review impact of each activity
- Grade by Level

Step 5 – Identify Opportunity Costs

- Assign value to your time
- Review activity for alternative solutions & new efficiencies
- Ask "Is the value of the outcome worth the time I will spend to do it?"
- Re-categorize activity Level, as needed

Step 6 – Build a Weekly Calendar

- Select 2-3 personal Level I activities per day
- Select 2-3 professional Level I activities per day
- Schedule only Level I activity on weekly calendar leaving buffer zones
- Revise and reschedule activity as necessary during the week

Chapter Five

Discovering Opportunity

*"The success always has a number of projects
planned, to which he looks forward. Any one of
them could change the course of his life overnight."*
— Mark Caine

It is said that opportunity doesn't knock twice. My experience indicates that it doesn't knock at all. Opportunity *is* everywhere—all around us, all of the time, but it never just comes "knocking". We must go to it, identify it, take some initiative, and make something of it.

Why is it so difficult for us to find? Because real opportunities are often the by-products of problem solving and trouble-shooting; they are frequently camouflaged as dilemmas or service issues. Because they do not command our immediate attention, mesmerizing busy work and established routines often obscure them. Because genuine opportunities are oddities. They are created in the realm of the unknown, developed in uncertainty, and refined beyond the confines of conventional wisdom. In our industry, new opportunities (such as new markets, new products and programs, and especially new services) spawn from new perspectives, new ideologies, and untested circumstances. Therefore, harvesting the opportunities requires us to disengage from current assumptions, activities, and habits, so that we are free to create and apply new ideas and behaviors to a new set of standards and conditions. Creatures of habit that we are, this is not easily done.

Comfort is a big opportunity killer. We are programmed to prefer the comfort of established routines and perspectives to anything foreign and mysterious. Our need to be comfortable is a survival impulse that causes us to be fearful of anything new and untested and it is responsible for an automatic rejection of new opinions, perspectives, and suggestions for behavior modification. Because change is difficult for people, because we succumb to change only when the pain of not changing becomes too much to bear or if we have no choice and are forced to change, genuine opportunities are often discovered on the tail end of crisis or catastrophe. Some of our greatest opportunities are sparked from the charred remains of ideas or circumstances gone bad simply because, smarting from a defeat, we are finally ready to see them.

Complacency is the shrewdest of all opportunity killers. Complacency lures us into believing that we need not change because who we are and what we are doing has worked and will continue to work. Complacency says "if it's not broken, don't fix it," almost always sacrificing genuine opportunities for familiar plays. Complacency convinces us that old routines can be successfully applied to new conditions and that we can continue to do what we do the way that we do it and fully expect to get different results. In reality, genuine opportunities are only developed when we are developing—when we are growing beyond our preconceptions and comfort zones.

A notable difference between an average producer and a top producer is the level of complacency apparent in their approach to work and to life. While each producer is equally capable of identifying a potential opportunity, top producers seize the initiative, apply some ingenuity, break through the commotion and clutter of business as usual—and cash in on the opportunity. Witnessing the success of the top producer, the average producer will often attribute his own lack of success to bad luck or unfair advantage, never realizing that if he would simply lift his head up from time to time, he could be just as successful.

Converting Opportunity

We are witnessing the beginning of a whole new Insurance Age. We are incredibly fortunate to be participants in this transformation because we are being given the chance to create something new and better rather than merely experiencing the legacy. The opportunities to come are as limitless as the stars and it is our generation that will be the first to explore them. Standing, as we are, on the cusp of what was and what will be, there has never been a better time to work in our industry. The price of entry is willingness—a willingness to look at what hasn't been looked at, try what hasn't been tried, and change when change is needed.

It should be obvious that new ideas require new initiatives to support them. To make room for the new endeavor, old behaviors must be altered or discarded all together, and priorities reestablished in favor of the new objectives. The greater the opportunity, the more radical the change that is required. The larger the opportunity, the more time and effort we have to invest to realize it. Ultimately, the price that we pay for our success is measured in energy, flexibility, and elbow grease.

Provided that they take the time to do it, most producers and service professionals that I've met can easily make a list of new and creative ideas that will launch them toward a new opportunity. Most of them can also take the next step and advance their ideas into a master plan. However, too few of them regularly muster enough sustained concentration to stick to their plan and convert opportunity into long-term prosperity. They simply lack the patience, discipline, and resolve to push beyond their need for immediate results and to remain unaffected by passing distractions.

This inability to create and adhere to a long-term vision imprisons people and organizations in an overly animated environment. Decisions are made and strategies are launched based upon temporary situations and transient information that is falsely interpreted to be permanent and fixed. Constantly reacting to the moment, in the moment, producers and their staff are unable to prioritize activity, synchronize it, and direct it at truly monumental opportunities.

Within companies that operate this way, it is rare to find business plans that stretch beyond the scope of convention to identify new and blatantly different market opportunities. Seldom do we see tactical marketing plans, sales plans, and service plans that are synchronized to ensure that every contact builds new opportunity upon the last. Infrequently do we find producers and service staff behaviors and psyches focused on anything other than the crisis of the moment, the work of the day, and the sale of the week. If these companies ever replaced their mission statements with reality statements, they would look something like this:

"As a traditional provider of insurance products to a vague and volatile market, we believe that we know all that we need to know about most things. What we know to be true today will always be true and what is working today will always work. We seek growth but not at the expense of change and we are firm believers in selling what we can, when we can, to whomever we can get to buy it. You can count on us to do the same thing in the same way, regardless of shifting needs or special circumstances."

Overcoming a company culture or personal selling process governed by conditioned responses and reactive thinking requires a more disciplined and systematic approach to attracting and retaining the right clients.

We must recognize that "selling" is a process that does not begin and end with "the transaction". As producers, we love to focus on the sale—the actual exchange—the conversion of prospects into clients. Even on our best days we have a tendency to rush or to want to rush through the preliminaries, the "courtship", and get to the sale. It is after all, our just reward, our redemption, and ... our nature. Sometimes in our haste to harvest we forget that each sales opportunity is unique with respect to the people involved, the process it must follow, and the time required for the relationship to develop.

Traditionally, we do a very good job with the perfunctory components of the sale. We collect the loss runs, review the policies, audit the reserves, design and shop the program, secure the best available price, and present our work like a technician. Focused as we are on product and price, we can easily forget that the most important, most dynamic, most unpredictable, and certainly the most fascinating attributes of the selling process are the relationships—the relationships between people who sell insurance and people who buy insurance. Ordinary people perhaps at first glance, but if you dig below the surface a bit you will find an extraordinary glossary of experiences, motives, values, behaviors, habits, beliefs, ambitions, fears, emotions, likes, and dislikes that all combine to form a unique selling environment with every sale.

Now, what happens when we pay lip service to the "nature" of the sale and focus instead on the facts and figures? We inadvertently signal that our primary interest is the completion of the deal and that the relationship will develop within the confines of the timeline that we have placed on the deal. We treat every client like every other client and incorrectly assume that because we know our trade, we know our traders. Sensing our lack of awareness and sensitivity, our clients treat us like a common peddler and their insurance program like a commodity.

Now let's put some pressure on the whole thing. Unlike every other financial advisor (attorney, accountant, banker, etc.) our relationship is up for grabs at every expiration date. Our clients would never consider shopping for legal services each year nor would they regularly bid out their corporate tax contract, yet every year we are faced with the very real risk of losing our clients to a competitor and, conversely, we are presented with the opportunity to gain clients from a competitor. Consumed as we can be with life's preoccupations and interruptions, the time that we can actually devote to selling and client service activities never seems to be enough. We are equally overwhelmed by the need to retain our existing book and by the need to add new clients whenever and wherever possible.

As we get increasingly anxious about adding new business, we get more "demanding" about binding business or getting a broker of record letter. The need for instant gratification (in the form of a sale) for the time and attention devoted to a prospect overwhelms the long-term advantages of patient and deliberate client acquisition. Urgency and emergency replace proactive client development and we set our sights on what appear to be easy targets— prospects that are nearing their expiration date and those that regularly bid. Following the herd of other producers during this, our hunting season, we struggle to differentiate, collect the policies and claims data, grab whatever market that we can, hastily prepare a proposal, and hope that ours is the one with the lowest price. We do it all in a flurry of activity and we do it all without ever truly getting to know our prospective client. Sometimes we win, most of the time ... we lose.

Another prospect gone bad.

Now hurry along to the next one.

Quickly now, before somebody else gets there first.

Hurry!

Quick!

Fast!

Move!

Gooooo!

Yuck.

And we do it all the time.

Even if we win the account we often lose. Accounts that come by bid will eventually go by bid. Accounts in motion tend to stay in motion due to service issues, financial difficulties, poor claims performance, and less than credible insurance buying practices.

No wonder we have earned such a poor reputation for integrity and sincerity. Frankly, our behavior validates the stereotype. We don't want to sell this way, none of us have to sell this way; but all of us, at one time or another, have been convinced that this is the right way. We are in dire need of a fresh perspective.

Shortcuts, quick pick-ups, and overnight successes are for package delivery companies and Hollywood starlets, not for insurance producers. Our success will be determined by our ability to identify lasting opportunity, establish a plan to capitalize on the opportunity, and discipline ourselves to carry out the plan. To avoid corruption, we must allow the opportunities to evolve naturally, patiently, and consistently. Our plan will be called a "marketing plan"; however, it will be unlike any marketing initiative that we have undertaken before and it will be dramatically different from the banal marketing tactics used by hit-and-run producers. Your plan will be custom-developed to communicate your message of integrity to a limited audience that is pre-selected to appreciate who you are and what you can do for them.

Insurance marketing programs go wrong because they start wrong. They correctly assume that opportunity is everywhere yet they incorrectly suppose that everyone is a potential opportunity.

Not everyone is qualified to be our client. One of the greatest challenges that we encounter as producers is learning how to distinguish the genuine opportunities from the multitude of vagabonds. Traditional marketing gimmicks actually exacerbate this problem by indiscriminately reaching out to saints and sinners alike.

Take for instance the cold call. I don't think that I have met any producer that really likes to make them and I know that I haven't met anyone that enjoys receiving them, yet many of us rely on this traditional technique to mine for opportunity in the marketplace. It is intrusive, inefficient, and discomforting for peddler and prospect alike. I remember my cold calling days as bad days made worse by the prospects that actually took the call.

Most of us have long since abandoned this intrusive practice in favor of a more palatable one. That said, I continue to find that a cold call *mentality* still dominates in a majority of producer marketing and prospecting systems. The premise of their strategy is that selling is a numbers game. Cast a wide net (through mass-mailers, telemarketers, advertisements, radio, etc.), reel it in, sort it out, and work frantically to find a keeper. Although this process generates an impressive amount of work, it does so at the cost of efficiency and it creates a selling environment that reeks of urgency and desperation. This numbers game does not and will not provide enough quality return for the time and attention invested. It simply creates too many unqualified exposures that are hastily and fruitlessly pursued as if they were real.

We are much better served by a calmer, more manageable system. We feel less pressure, client selection improves, and integrity is established as a way of doing business. Recognizing that there is a more appropriate way to conduct ourselves is a vital first step toward truly making the transition. Following up the change-of-heart with a determined effort to replace the old behaviors, however, is where the work and the real challenge begins.

I have anything but fond recollections of my leap from the old school to my new life. Breaking well-established habits is one thing; doing so while trying to immediately adopt an entirely new set of behaviors is quite another. Similar, I think, to swearing off a native language prior to learning a foreign one. This struggle is comparable to the experience that I described in the section about Goal Setting in Chapter 3.

Developing fresh ideas and creating an innovative marketing strategy was fairly simple—consistently executing the strategy seemed impossible. Rather than synchronizing and simplifying my activity, the new plan seemed as cumbersome and inefficient as the old. The results that I expected didn't materialize and my level of distress was as high as ever before. I was sending out letters, hosting roundtables, conducting workshops, writing articles, giving speeches, shaking hands, and kissing babies. Nothing was materializing—it all seemed like a huge waste of time and effort.

Ready to give up, I seriously considered a career move. The old way sucked and the new way didn't work. I wanted a fast out. Of course I had to clear such a move with my wife and, after listening patiently to my impasse, she delivered another blow that would change my life.

"The only thing I see that isn't working is you," she said. "Your expectations are way out of whack, Scott, and you are trying to apply old thinking to a new set of circumstances. For as long as I've known you, you have been a cyclone of activity. Always in a rush, always balancing multiple priorities, laptops, cell phones, appointments, and heavy traffic. Always in motion—on your way from some place, to some place. Never do you pause, sit still, and wait, for anything. Have you ever wondered what you are running from? Have you ever really considered what it is that you are running so hard to catch?"

"What the ...?" is all I came up with.

Sensing my confusion and knowing me well enough to recognize the first signs of temper tantrum, she set off down a gentler path.

"We all face a variety of situations everyday that require us to act. Some things demand fast action, others require a more deliberate, pensive approach. Most things fall somewhere in between. You, my love, apply fast action to all circumstances, all of the time. Everything is <u>NOW</u>, including your expectations about what the results of your actions should be and when they should appear. You have designed a marketing plan that requires organized, systematic, pause-reflect-adjust thinking and execution in order for it to prove effective. That is not who you are or how you work. The plan is fine—you are broken."

I mumbled something, probably an expletive, and she continued.

"The way I see it, you have two options. Option 1- return to your old system that you hate and don't change a thing or, Option 2—recognize what is holding you back and decide that it is time to evolve. If you choose to change,

the first step is to let go of the fears and insecurity that cause you to rush, panic, and act out of desperation. You know this fear well, Scott. So well, in fact, it controls your every move. Your fear of not getting there first, your fear of losing out, and your fear of not measuring up. Your fear of not getting something you want and your fear of not keeping what you have. The cure for your fear, Scott, is faith. Faith that doing the right thing in the right way with the right people for the right reasons will yield the right result. Faith in your ability, faith in your integrity, faith in your plan, and faith in those of us that support you."

Words cannot describe how much I did not want to hear this. Nonetheless, she was rolling and I was listening.

"Once your faith is established and your fear is quieted, you can hear the signals that your soul is sending and act accordingly. You will understand that a right opportunity is not fleeting; it is forever. You will work systematically and deliberately, focusing your attention and directing your energy on the process rather than being consumed by the expected result."

"It will become obvious that your process must begin by identifying a manageable population of carefully profiled prospective clients who are worthy and wanting of the time and attention that you will devote to them. Your approach to the market will be careful, considerate, credible, unique, and highly personalized, because you are building relationships rather than pushing product or price."

"You will abandon the insanity of the "fetch and close" mentality and replace it with an earnest desire to consistently provide your clients with enough information to make an educated decision, regardless of the time it will take for them to make this decision. You will feel better about who you are, what you do, and how you do it because you are treating people the way you wish to be treated. You will learn to accept the way things should be rather than constantly struggling to have them your way."

"You will redefine the meaning of success in terms that you can't even imagine exist today and you will accomplish more than you have ever dreamed possible. It is a simple choice to make, Scott, but not an easy one. Now, what's it going to be?"

Gulp. What would you say?

I am so grateful for my wife, her insight, her bravery, and for this verbal kick-in-the-ass. I went back to work and, for the first time, I really started working right. It took years of wrestling with the ghosts of bad habits before I truly began to experience all of the sensations that she described and, even today, I must be constantly on guard against fear, doubt, insecurity, and the havoc that they can induce. My journey to success was not a straight shot to the top of the heap. It proved to be a long and crooked path that still has no end in sight. Life and the challenges that come with it didn't get any easier; however, I learned to accept life on life's terms and I learned to take it easier. Things in life didn't get better—I got better.

This lesson and the personal transition that followed is certainly a defining moment in my life. I am thrilled by the thought that you too might benefit by it and one day share with me your own story. The marketing concepts that follow are all a product of this new approach. Prior to moving on, please consider the following:

- Desperation is sinister. It causes us to behave in ways that we would not even consider when our confidence is intact. Worse yet, it is hard to hide and is usually apparent to all who come into contact with it, particularly prospective clients. To view a demonstration of what it can look like, rent a copy of the movie *Glenngary, Glennross* on your next visit to the video store. Desperation doesn't stand a chance against hope and progress, both of which result from working an established plan in a meaningful way.

- You will find that the easiest people to talk to and meet with are usually those that waste your time. The problem with cold calls and other intrusive marketing schemes is that you attract people who respond to these tactics. You have to wonder what is inspiring them.

- Timing really is everything. However, finding the right place to be is a necessary first step to being there at the right time. Successful marketing plans begin with detailed market research and an accurate cost/benefit analysis. It's usually boring, time consuming, and often expensive. It sometimes yields results that contradict our initial assumptions and inform us that our good idea isn't so good after all. Good research can be a spoiler, but it can also save your ass. Although most producers avoid it due to the downside, those that deliberately quantify and qualify the real opportunity are able to draw a direct line to it, efficiently retrieve it, and be home before dark—while everyone else is still wandering around.

- Opportunity is a moving target that must be tracked and captured. Any guide will tell you that each hunt brings new opportunity and new challenges along with it; no two are ever the same. Successful hunters rely on their previous experience and wisdom to overcome the challenges that they face and seize the opportunity that results. You are no different. Enjoy the safari.

> *"You, yourself, have got to see that there is no just interpretation of life except in terms of life's best things. No pleasure philosophy, no sensuality, no place nor power, no material success can for a moment give such inner satisfaction as the sense of living for good purposes, for maintenance of integrity, for the preservation of self-approval."*
> —Minot Simons, D.D.

Chapter Six:

Channel Marketing — Breaking Through the Hullabaloo

"When an archer misses the mark he turns and looks for the fault within himself. Failure to hit the bull's-eye is never the fault of the target. To improve your aim, improve yourself."
— Gilbert Arland

The Trouble with Legacy Marketing

A wise sage once said that the success of a business doesn't depend on its size. It depends on filling a void in the marketplace. Consider 7-11, the convenience store chain known for its easy access and piping hot coffee. Sure, 7-11 isn't going to take market share away from a Pathmark or a Stop 'n Shop, or any other national grocery store chain. Then again, neither will the big grocery stores compete successfully with 7-11. Each serves different needs.

Let's face it. Serving a customer's specific needs is what business is all about. Sometimes that's best done in a multi-million dollar marketing campaign, like Apple Computers did in 1999 when it rolled its iMac computers to great commercial success. Or it can be as simple as selling yourself on a one-on-one basis, much like financial planner Fritz Brauner did some years ago at a conference he was attending. Frustrated by weak response from potential customers, Brauner changed his nametag from "Financial Planner" to "Money" and soon found himself surrounded by customers.

Both 7-11 and Brauner succeeded because they knew their customers. As Peter Drucker once said: "The aim of marketing is to know and understand your client so well that the product or service you offer literally sells itself." Effectively communicating a message that is attractive enough to draw the client companies to you, ahead of all others is, by far, the greatest barrier to success you'll ever face in your sales career. Am I being overly dramatic? Hardly. There's so much marketing clutter out there it's difficult to know what to do. Here's what we do know. We know that the insurance industry is constantly bombarding our prospects with presumptuous marketing litter. We also know that despite their claims, they all sound alike, act alike, and even look alike. Finally, we know that most are only truly interested in converting clients to cash as quickly as possible.

This commonality of message and behavior is one of our industry's greatest deficiencies. What does that mean to us? Plenty, as it turns out. Our plan is designed to expose this opening and exploit it by debunking conventional marketing practices and creating new ways to position you properly in the marketplace.

As I've mentioned already, our industry needs a fresh message and a new approach to marketing, especially when it comes to promoting its greatest asset—you. Impersonal, broad-based, traditional approaches to "getting things sold" are usually designed to announce a special program, price, product, or service. Generally categorized as mass marketing, these methods inadvertently portray insurance as a commodity and, by default, promote insurance buying practices that are price and product focused. Unable or unwilling to distinguish one producer from another in a seemingly unlimited pool of providers, the client establishes a buying process that mirrors the selling characteristics of the industry. They create a proposal package for each bidder, make it available 90 days ahead of the expiration date, cover the markets, and hunt for the low cost provider. That means you, the producer, are only considered as an intermediary, a necessary middleman whose only function is to complete the transaction.

It's not that the client wishes producers entirely out of the picture. They just don't truly know the importance of having a really good one. Consequently, beyond securing a desirable market, little consideration is given to the potential impact of the producer/agency/client relationship. Clients have learned to expect limited or no post-sale producer contact and resign themselves to reactive, problem-based, administrative service from carriers and agency personnel that they have never met.

Frankly, if clients could shop and buy their commercial policies over the phone or through the internet and avoid the annual buying circus, they would. One needs only to look at the term-life, auto, and small group arena for an illustration.

Consider for a moment the junk mail that clutters up your mailbox. How much do you get and how much do you actually read? Probably plenty and none, respectively. To trick you into opening their junk mail, direct mail houses have actually started concealing their mailings in blank envelopes. What is your state-of-mind when you open it? Closed, probably. Most likely you are skeptical, slightly annoyed, and looking for "the catch". If and when you do respond, what is your motivation for doing so? In most instances a special deal, a discount, or a novelty—in essence price and/or product might cause you to respond. Do you expect anything more? Usually not. The same can be said for the people that respond to our mailings and cold calls.

Let's keep things civil and say that these customers are not exactly the pick of the litter. The majority of them are shopping for a bargain, not a buddy. Quite often they are on the verge of being non-renewed or canceled for one reason or another, frequently due to a poor loss history or for failure to pay their premiums. Either way, these clients are transients. Be wary when they contact you and keep your guard up. Chances are such clients won't be with you for long—regardless of what you do or don't do.

Unfortunately, in our industry, mass marketing usually nets only squandered resources, fruitless follow-up, and wasted exposures to people and organizations that may or may not be good prospects. Under normal circumstances, mass marketing usually gets us in front of people we don't want or who don't want us. That's a recipe for disaster for producers.

What's the solution? Simple. It's time to junk the horizontal approach and get vertical. In an era of hard-to-find premium dollars and stiff competition, the average agency or broker is better served by a more deliberate, less expensive, carefully targeted marketing effort that sells you to the people you want to be sold to and affords you the time to service your current book of business. Remember that a good marketing campaign allows you to keep what you have and get you what you don't have. That's the objective of a personalized marketing system—to reach out and captivate a limited group of carefully selected clients who recognize and value what you have to offer and are worthy of your time and attention.

When implemented, your marketing strategy represents a significant split from what is considered by your clients to be normal and expected behavior. Historically, sales objectives and marketing strategies evolve from a pre-occupation with converting clients to cash in the shortest time possible. In this scenario, the selling process is a game of ratios. The motive is self-serving, the approach is intrusive, and the clients are not fooled by the vanity. They know the game.

By concentrating on you and how you can help the clients you're targeting, your strategy starts different and stays different. Eventually, your clients will recognize that you are truly sincere and come to appreciate the value, integrity, and trust that you provide. However, it will take time to break through the layers of presumption and skepticism that defend against the pretenders. The key, as you'll soon see, is putting that time to good use.

Introducing Channel Marketing

Channel marketing has nothing to do with your TV clicker, although becoming more visible is certainly part of the plan. In the insurance industry, channel marketing occurs when agencies and producers within an agency strategically identify a commercial niche or market, develop an expertise in that market, and specialize in satisfying the risk management and loss control needs of that market.

Such "specialization" causes a "snowball effect". As a producer's proficiency in and exposure to the industry evolves, so too will that producer's reputation. Alliances within the market will grow to such a degree that they create a virtual monopoly and own that niche. Carriers scramble to assemble special programs, potential clients are referred in, trade journals and associations want to know more; integrity and expertise become the calling card. Successful producers who have consistently out-performed all others have done so by employing this strategy earnestly, honestly, systematically, and thoroughly.

Why is channel marketing so effective?

Call it the herd mentality. Just as individuals within a specific group exhibit common tendencies, organizations engaged concurrently in an industry or association will also demonstrate group characteristics.

These market characteristics lead customers to act similarly in their affiliations, buying habits, opinions, and methods of operation. A customer will be more comfortable and receptive to you, above all others, if you demonstrate an unmistakable awareness of who he is, what he does, how he does it, and can help him do it better.

Having established your credibility in a myriad of industry venues, customers will seek you out based upon your expertise and the recommendation of others within the industry. Your competitors, usually perceived as generalists, will be pressured out of the market or not permitted entry because of your value and proficiency as an industry specialist, i.e. someone who is perceived by the customer as one who can solve a particular problem better than anyone else.

How do you select a market?

Time for a look in the mirror. That's because your initial step in determining which market to approach should be an informal self-evaluation. Remember how skeptical potential customers can be—many suspect that, given a choice, your interests will outweigh theirs every time. As a result, your success in the market that you select will be rooted in your sincere desire to help and advise, not to exploit and manipulate. Your motive must be service oriented, steeped in an honest desire to make the industry better for your presence. Also remember what you are marketing—your expertise and ingenuity. Then there's your ability to reduce a client's long-term insurance cost by designing and implementing custom-developed, proactive risk management and loss control programs. You are not marketing insurance or your ability to sell it. The relationships that you establish within the market will be based upon these differences and these are preconditions that cannot be simulated.

Plenty of sharks swim in these deep waters. It's hardly a secret that the market is full of marauders and specialists of the month whose motive is simply to make a sale. The shallow interest that they exhibit in the market is clearly apparent to most customers, who find their presence offending and intrusive, thus making your job that much more difficult. In the end, your honesty and strong ethics will be the difference-maker. Because you will be perceived by a potential customer as different only if you honestly are, your selection of a "specialty" should be based upon who you are and where your interests lie. It helps to know something about the class of business and the industry before you begin.

Also, try to find a market that is not excessively prospected by other producers looking to specialize. You'll recall the beginning of this chapter where I alluded to the small convenience store and the big grocery chain. "Specialization" explains how a big supermarket and small convenience store can survive and thrive on the same block. Both generate profits in separate ways. The giant grocer offers variety at low prices. The convenience store provides constant access to highly-sought after goods like milk and bread at high prices. While both exist on the same block, they prosper because they each fill different needs. In the insurance sector, most "attractive" markets are big targets with an abundance of snipers. Why take on that much competition? Instead, be creative in selecting your niche and choose a market that is stable, proven, growing, and populated. If a territory limits you, the target population within the geographical boundary must be significant; otherwise it could be a waste of valuable time, energy, and resources.

Selecting the niche that works for you is easier said than done, right? It's difficult to find fertile ground these days. Insurance companies have long understood the inherent value in targeting industry specific clients with specialty programs. As a result, you might find it difficult to gain prominence in a market segment that has been inundated with similar claims to fame. If this is the case, select instead a non-industry specific segment of the middle market that will value your risk management and loss control initiatives.

Consider the following examples. Keep in mind that these Pennsylvania agencies all operate within 20 miles of each other, they each have but a single location, and all are wildly successful. Not one of them participates in traditional marketing practices to attract new clients. Instead they rely on referrals, networking, and their reputations for providing integrity, value, and trust.

The Graham Company – Philadelphia, PA

(Marketing Strategy – select, high-end, complex accounts)

Founded in 1950 by William A. Graham, III, the firm began as a small insurance agency. In 1968, with six employees and a premium volume of $500,000, William A. Graham, IV, began purchasing the stock of the company from his father, becoming sole owner in 1972.

Today, The Graham Company remains closely held and has a team of 175 employees directly involved with the Property - Casualty - Surety end of the business. Premium volume for 1997 was approximately $100,000,000. In 1997, the company was ranked as the 48th largest insurance broker in the United States. This record of success is all the more remarkable in that the growth of The Graham Company has been accomplished without any of the mergers and acquisitions that have come to characterize the industry.

The fact that The Graham Company is ranked among the top 50 insurance brokers in the nation becomes more impressive considering that the company serves fewer than 200 clients. Agencies of similar ranking serve on average, more than 2,500 clients. This disparity is intentional and strategic. The Graham Company's clients are an elite group of industry leaders with complex insurance and risk management needs. Their clients demand and obtain superior account management and unparalleled service.

Over the years, The Graham Company has formed strong client relationships with market leaders in a broad range of industries, including construction, high technology, food processing, manufacturing, energy, healthcare, municipalities, and international distribution.

The Graham Company primarily works with clients who run well-managed, financially strong businesses. These are usually closely held companies—both public and private—where the principal shareholders have a vested interest in the quality of their property and casualty insurance program. Each client is unique, defined by complex concerns, long-term goals, and a realistic corporate culture.

The Addis Group – King of Prussia, PA

(Marketing Strategy – Select, middle-market, risk management receptive accounts)

The history of the Addis Group is a remarkable success story within the insurance industry; a story of growth through service and client satisfaction that is unparalleled and truly visionary.

The Addis group was founded in 1990 with the belief that helping clients to maximize the value of their insurance programs involved much more than shopping around for the cheapest price. Knowing that proactive risk management and loss control policies and practices create a formidable barrier to rising insurance costs, The Addis Group worked with clients to develop workplace safety education and training programs, emergency and disaster plans, consistent employment practices, and cost effective claims and disability case management.

Prior to making any recommendations regarding insurance products, The Addis Group conducts a comprehensive risk management assessment of the organization, its culture, and its people. Rather than simply gathering underwriting data to prepare a bid, members of the assessment team conduct a thorough needs analysis that includes employee interviews, facilities inspections, job safety analysis, and a host of other specific audits.

Upon completing the assessment, a written report of findings and recommendations is provided to the management team for review. This is all done free of charge and long before specific policies and rates are discussed. As a result, The Addis Group has evolved into one of the premier risk management consultants and insurance brokers in the region.

Today, it oversees the group insurance and risk management needs of more than 600 diverse businesses, representing over $50 million in premium or premium equivalents.

Palley-Simon Associates – Jenkintown, PA

(Marketing Strategy – Public and Private Schools and Universities)

Palley-Simon insures more schools than any other insurance agency in Pennsylvania. Their demonstrated success at penetrating, capturing, and owning the school market is a textbook example of how target marketing can and does work in a highly competitive environment.

Beginning in 1975, Palley-Simon initiated a comprehensive examination of insurance buying practices in public school systems. Their year-long investigation uncovered monumental inconsistencies in "standard" coverage, significant deficiencies in risk management programs, and excessive worker's compensation rates.

Enlisting the help of a panel of experts, Samuel Palley custom-developed a comprehensive school system program that included proactive risk management programs and the state's first self-insured worker's compensation pool.

Since its inception, the original program has been considerably revised and enhanced to keep pace with the growing needs of the market. What hasn't changed is Palley-Simon's commitment to providing Pennsylvania schools with unsurpassed insurance programs and risk management expertise.

To date, Palley-Simon manages the insurance needs of 80 school systems in the greater Philadelphia area and controls a whopping 20% of the total available market statewide.

How do you approach the market?

Marketing yourself as an expert requires more than grabbing a bull-horn and mounting a soapbox. You can try it, but self-promotion isn't enough to claim fame as an industry expert or risk management special-ist. It's better to be known for your expertise by demonstrating to the members of the market your ability to creatively develop new solutions to existing problems and identify future opportunities and potential hazards. "I fix cars" is one thing. But "I fix cars affordably and deliver them to your home" or "I fix Ferraris better than anyone else" is something else altogether. Take a deep breath and recognize that this is a process and not an event. A process that begins with your education. The general regimen to follow is this: having identified your channel market, go where they go, do what they do, read what they read, and listen when they talk. Listen really well.

Also, get used to the notion that up is down and down is up—it's what helps split you from the herd. The traditional approach to selling is to attempt the sale first and then build a relationship with those who buy. In channel marketing this process is reversed so that our motive is better served. We seek first to build a relationship with selected prospects and maintain the relationship with service initiatives normally reserved for post-sale account management. Sales opportunities will naturally develop and occur as our value to the industry becomes more entrenched. Our value to the market will be correlated with our understanding of the specific needs and concerns faced by the industry and our ability to respond.

Be careful how you frame those needs. Client needs must be defined from the client's point of view, not from your perceptions of the issues or any assumptions that you might be inclined to make. Again, some due diligence is the key. The needs of your market can be determined by reading trade journals and risk management reports, conducting informational interviews with market members, studying industry trends, reviewing claims data and regulatory rulings, attending association meetings, and by surveying cen-ters-of-influence within the market.

Simply stated, a center-of-influence is "an individual or organiza-tion with strength of character and recognized leadership in your channel market". They tend to be more progressive and profitable than most others within their industry. The mention of a center-of-influence's name will elicit a positive response from most prospects within their market. Why? Because success is respected and people want to be identified with suc-cess. My travels throughout the U.S. reveal an interesting view on success.

Go to New York and you'll obviously see a lot of Yankee fans. No surprise there. But go to Salt Lake City, Toledo, or Sacramento and you'll find a lot of Yankee fans, too. Why? Because historically, they're winners (as a Red Sox fan I'm grinding my teeth as I write these words). It's not an isolated occurrence. During Michael Jordan's reign with the Chicago Bulls, it was not uncommon to walk down the streets of Tokyo or Milan and see those familiar red jerseys with the number "23" on the back and the word "Bulls" on the front. People of all nationalities saw Jordan as a winner and hence, wanted to "Be Like Mike".

The thinking goes, if you are affiliated with that success, you too will share that respect. Industry members and market observers hold opinions from centers-of-influence in high regard. Your relationship with the centers-of-influence within your market will ultimately determine your level of acceptance and integrity within the industry.

Your initial contact with the channel market and the centers-of-influence should be systematic, professional, and consistent. Do nothing in big volumes, a bad idea for an efficiency-seeking producer. Understand that any attempt to overwhelm the market with glossy marketing stuff will be perceived as stereotypical and prove counter-productive. Your motive must be to support, service, and provide information to the market. Every contact with the industry should bolster this effort. In essence, you are treating your potential clients as if they were already clients by providing consistent demonstrations of your value and commitment.

In this successful and unique marketing strategy, you are investing in your clients before asking them to invest in you and thus proving yourself to be legitimate.

Here is your objective—to create a system for providing service that is manageable and unique. No worries—I'll help you do it. Just review and use the ideas on the pages that follow, adjust them to match up with you and your market, and design your own plan. Remember that the key to success in any channel marketing system is consistent exposure to organizations and individuals that need and want what you have to offer. Take the time to plan a deliberate and disciplined approach.

I can't emphasize that point enough. Successful marketing to a target industry takes time, patience, diligence, and an honest desire to help. You will be successful if your approach is focused on building and maintaining long-term client relationships by consistently and measurably providing risk management and loss control solutions to the market and by establishing your role in this accomplishment. Once installed as the agent of choice for your professional, consultative, and informed approach to the industry, you are untouchable. Just "like Mike".

Beginning at the Beginning

A thorough channel marketing system consists of at least three non-selling approaches that are implemented simultaneously and consistently. On the pages that follow you will find outlines and sample systems to use in gaining exposure to your selected market. However, prior to starting any marketing effort, make sure that you have adequately addressed the following:

Selecting The Market:

   a) On the basis of your prior knowledge and your ability to help and inform.
   b) Not excessively prospected by other producers.
   c) Present and populated in your geographic nest.
   d) Will respect and value proactive risk management practices.

Researching The Market:

   a) Analyze existing and historical trends, habits, and needs.
   b) Determine what markets and carrier programs are available.
   c) Estimate average premium to ensure targets are large enough.
   d) Review trade, industry, and association publications.
   e) Search the internet for industry newsletters and risk management articles.
   f) Identify key prospects and centers-of-influence.

Marketing Plan Design

   a) Targeted to a small, select group of prospects.
   b) Planned for low volume, consistent, monthly touches.
   c) Must be professional, highly personalized, and service-based.
   d) Should be easy to administer.

Researching Your Market

1) Determine your market and select a sales objective indicated by number of accounts or value of premium.

2) Create a top 25-50 prospect list for your market with key contact names, addresses, and phone numbers. This information is readily available from list providers such as Info USA, Imarket, Judy Diamond, etc. The required information may also be obtained from:

   a) Chambers of Commerce.

   b) The internet.

   c) Association membership rosters.

   d) Existing clients.

   e) Public library business directories.

   f) Trade journals and industry publications.

We strongly encourage you to invest in some type of computer-based contact management system such as ACT, Goldmine, Maximizer, etc. Any of these products will help manage your data and your activity with efficiency and consistency.

3) Obtain a list of trade journals and industry associations. All journals and associations have web sites that you should visit.

   a) Request subscription information.

   b) Request a sample copy.

   c) Request publishing guidelines for articles.

   d) Build a database noting publication address and editor.

4) Interview current clients within your target market and conduct a detailed assessment of industry needs and common risk management concerns. Also review trade journals, risk management articles, web articles, and association publications. You are looking for new and developing issues that encompass all lines of coverage, including employment practices, general and product liability, workers compensation, group and voluntary benefits, insurance buying practices, etc. Record each issue and trend.

   Set daily and weekly reading and interview objectives.

5) Find out which carriers are currently insuring the market, what programs are available, and what risk management and loss control services are being provided. Ask specifically about the risk characteristics of the industry, claims history, and underwriting criteria. What makes for a good risk and why?

6) Based on the industry assessment, brainstorm for potential solutions to each identifiable need. Indicate the source of the solution, action required, and the positive effect of implementing the resolution. Seek the input of carriers, industry specialists, and centers-of-influence. Don't forget to include the savings associated with the "soft effect" of your solutions. For example:

   a) Reduced employee turnover.

   b) Improved morale.

   c) Increased productivity.

   d) Improved quality.

   e) Enhanced customer service.

7) Establish an industry clipping file to hold pertinent information about the market and its members. Regularly search the internet for new information, stay in touch with centers-of-influence, sweep the trade journals, etc. If your channel market is geographically based rather than industry specific, keep a careful watch for news regarding the companies that appear on your prospect list. This includes both good and bad news.

Your research does not end here. In fact, it never ends. You can never, ever know enough about your market. As the industry expert, you must have a firm foundation to cement your expertise. Your ongoing education is the cornerstone of this foundation.

Approaching the market

Having selected and properly researched your targeted niche, it is now appropriate to professionally approach the market from the perspective of an industry observer and partner. You have in hand all that you will need to effectively differentiate. Your research has provided you with your market's specific needs and now it is time to gradually and systematically convert their need into your opportunity. Your method for doing so is informative rather than intrusive, solution-based rather than sales driven.

The objective of your marketing effort is to provide your prospects with enough information to make an educated decision about who you are and what you do. Remember, your message should convey professionalism, specialization, and your desire to provide a service—not to sell a product.

Your system is designed to ensure consistent exposure to the market over time and your method for doing so will be personalized, honorable, and manageable. Try employing three or more of the following systems simultaneously:

Approach Methods for Channel Marketing

1. Pre-Approach Letters (See samples below)
2. Newsletters (paper & electronic)
3. Roundtables
4. Associations
5. Networking
6. Referrals
7. Article Publications
8. Centers-of-Influence
9. Focus Groups
10. Safety Seminars and Risk Management Workshops
11. Speeches
12. Clipping Files (paper & electronic)

Pre-Approach Letters

Cold calls are like root canals. Dentists don't like doing them and patients don't like getting them.

Even so, producers continue to waste time trying to get through to prospects that have no known need for their service, hoping to grab lightning in a bottle and catch them at the precise moment they may be feeling the need for a change and are ready to listen to another agent. The success rate for this approach is dismal due to the intrusive nature of the contact. As we have already discussed, your time is better served by talking with those who already know who you are and what you do.

Instead, plant a few seeds first and watch them yield bountiful results. Using a personalized pre-approach letter in advance of a telephone call to convey your message, mention your expertise or specialization, and inform the prospect that you will be calling to follow up, removes the element of surprise and creates a warmer reception. Now, when you do call, you're no longer the stranger; the intrusive maker of cold calls. Instead, you're the familiar—or at least recognizable—maker of follow-up calls. Here, the client is aware that you will be calling, they know why you're calling, and they can make an educated decision whether or not to accept or return your call. Not only is this approach less intrusive and far more professional, the time spent chasing prospects who would rather avoid you is greatly diminished.

Not everyone is a fan of laying the groundwork before calling. Opponents of pre-approach letters and follow-up systems often base their opinion on past mailings that have met with little or no success. But don't forsake the medium for the message. After reviewing samples of these letters I often find that the message, not the messenger, was to blame. Here is a short list of the most common errors found in failed pre-approach systems:

Motive:

The objective of any pre-approach letter should only be to introduce you, your agency, your specialty, and the fact that you will be calling in a few days to follow up. It is not intended to get an appointment, make a sale, or to have the potential client call you.

Length:

Studies conducted on what gets read all indicate that the most effective business letter is: concise, direct, personalized, and bulleted.

We often find that producers have attempted to convey far too much technical information about a product rather than focus on the specific benefits of a service. Remember that this letter is only intended to be a preliminary introduction. We suggest limiting your letter to one or two simple and direct paragraphs. There will be plenty of opportunities later on to get specific.

Follow-up:

Perhaps the greatest stumbling block of them all is the tendency to try to do too much too soon. Our letters are not mass mailings. They are personalized introductions that must be followed up with a phone call in a timely manner. For that reason, we should stagger the mailings and limit the volume to ensure proper follow-up.

Try these suggestions for designing your pre-approach letter and delivery system so it works.

Your letter should be:

- Personalized and mailed directly to the decision-maker. Don't start with the gate guard by addressing it to "Attn: CEO". That's just a guarantee that it won't make it to the CEO.

- Brief and easy to read (One Page Maximum!). Hemingway was on to something when he said "brevity is key". Use bullets to highlight key points. Leave out any reference to competitive pricing or claims of superior service. You cannot accurately establish your value for the client until you have asked the client to define value.

- Crystal clear in purpose. Your intention is only to introduce who you are, what you do, and to inform the recipient that you will be calling to follow-up.

- Signed by you and include one sheet of testimonials, references, or benefits.

Your system should be:

- Manageable and Consistent. This is not a mass-mailing or marketing effort. You will need to follow up on every letter sent. Prepare a fixed number of letters per day or per week and schedule your phone calls for a specific time and day.

- Planned for contingencies in advance. Each contact that you make will lead to an appointment, a request for additional information, a continuance, an advance, or a no. Regardless of the result, each contact should trigger another letter (see examples in the Online Library located at: www.gopolestar.com). Remember that we are building relationships based upon our ability to respond and you should be prepared to respond to every call or attempt.

- Written out on a Goal Planning Sheet and known by your service and support team. Set a weekly objective for mailings and follow-up phone calls.

The following are two examples of pre-approach letters that effectively cut against the grain of the legacy marketing systems. Additional letters can be found in the Online Library.

Pre-approach Letter I (Anti-Marketing Theme)

Dear Contact:

This letter is only one of many that you will receive during the year from a variety of insurance agencies requesting a look at your policies. Most will trumpet competitive rates, good service, and a dedicated staff. Few, if any, will actually deliver and none will dare to proactively venture beyond the issues of policies and rates to thoroughly understand your organizational culture and unique needs. To do so requires an honest demonstration of an agency's commitment and capability in advance of selling you insurance.

Our method of protecting you and the financial health of your company does not begin and end with the purchase of insurance. At *The Agency*, we refuse to use the old models and outdated techniques that are designed to generalize a business, feed it standard insurance, and then vanish until renewal time. We know that you deserve more and we are prepared to give it ... up front and without reservation.

Attached you will please find a brief description of our agency and our process. Our record proves that this value-driven approach leads to enhanced program design, reduced premiums, and satisfied clients.

In the near future, we will call you to formally introduce ourselves and we will do so with the knowledge that our process is not for everybody. On the other hand, if you are weary and leery of conventional agency limitations, ours would be a good call to take. In the interim, please feel free to call me directly with any questions or comments.

Sincerely,

Pre-approach Letter II (Article Enclosed)

Dear Contact:

Getting our message through to you is a tremendous challenge for our agency. I know that you are constantly targeted by insurance "salespeople" professing to be bigger, better, faster, or cheaper. I know that their marketing tactics are often intrusive, rarely unique, and very impersonal. I also know that despite their affirmations, they are largely interested in what you can do for them. I am as offended by the lack of sincerity as you are and I can certainly appreciate why you might be skeptical of our approach. I only hope that you might take a moment to consider our ideas before you make up your mind.

During the past year, we have witnessed significant rate increases across all lines of business. Next year, we anticipate that this pricing action will continue. Feeling powerless, many insureds begrudgingly consented to the increased cost of insurance without first inspecting all available alternatives. I want to make sure that this oversight is corrected and not repeated.

We use a unique method with our existing clients to avoid this issue and I am offering our services to you without cost. Our agency has developed a comprehensive assessment tool that we use to evaluate every component of your health, safety, and risk management concerns, as well as your organizational development and corporate cultural issues. This process is conducted onsite by our team of specialists, free of charge, and provides us with the knowledge necessary to make qualified recommendations regarding your risk management, loss control, and insurance programs. Far from being a gimmick, our record proves that this bold approach leads to enhanced program design, reduced premiums, and stabilized insurance costs—even in a rising market.

The enclosed article from ___, a leading industry publication, does a good job in explaining how our proactive philosophy and unique approach will benefit our clients. I know that you are skeptical; however, if you are even marginally curious, I encourage you to investigate us further. In the near future, we will call you to formally introduce ourselves. In the interim, please feel free to call me directly with any questions, comments, or for additional information.

Sincerely,

Newsletters

Newsletters are a magnificent way to establish credibility and market awareness, but only if they are written well and consistently published. Since we live in an eworld, electronic newsletters sent using e-mail are perhaps the easiest and most reliable method for creating and consistently sending newsletters. That said, printed newsletters continue to be the most popular because they are tangible and more readable. After all, you can't drag your computer—even a laptop—comfortably into bed with you at night when engaging in some light reading.

Production-wise, a four panel, quarterly publication is the most common format used, though a simple, two-sided, 8 1/2 x 11-inch single sheet is often just as effective. Your newsletter can serve the dual purpose of staying in touch with existing clients and, with the addition of a customized pre-approach letter, provide you with another avenue for introducing yourself to new prospects. Some suggestions for publication are as follows:

- The newsletter will be read if the selected topic is pertinent and the layout is attractive. Even electronic newsletters should be designed well. Review your list of market needs for topical information; this is an ideal forum to present your ideas. Focus on risk management solutions and examples of effective loss control programs that are specific to the market or specialty. Claims stories and investigation techniques are always interesting. If you do not have suitable software or if you are limited in your graphic design ability, "canned" newsletter services are available for a fee. Check the internet for the graphics and software that you need, and for design ideas. Most software packages such as Microsoft Word™ come with newsletter templates and enough instruction to get you going.

- Contact centers-of-influence and request an interview to include in the newsletter. Inform them that the interview will be published in your newsletter and permit them to discuss any topic of interest to the market, regardless of whether or not the discussion is insurance related. Ask them for recommendations regarding future topics and to identify other potential interviewees. Permit them to review a draft copy prior to publication. Also, ask for the names and addresses of organizations and individuals that should receive a copy.

- The newsletter is written for the market and should be about the market. Avoid the urge to sell or introduce new services. You can, however, designate space to welcome new clients, announce workshops, and introduce new employees. Also, feel free to highlight any meaningful testimonials or success stories that clients pass along, providing permission to do so is obtained prior to publishing.

- Design a pre-approach letter for prospects and personally contact them for feedback. Request an appointment to discuss your specialization in the market, how you service your clients, and to conduct an interview for a future newsletter.

- As mentioned, your newsletter is an efficient method for keeping in contact with your current clients, centers-of-influence, and top prospects. You can also use the newsletter to conduct a survey of your clients.

- Your newsletter must be planned proactively. Plan out each step in detail on a goal planning sheet and ensure all contributors and support people are familiar with the importance of the deadline. Once the first one is done, it must keep on being done. It is always best to be working one issue ahead of the current edition.

Roundtables

Camelot it's not, but the idea is the same. A roundtable brings members and observers of the market together to discuss issues, events, problems, and ideas that are risk management related. Your motive in hosting a roundtable is relationship-centered and not sales-related. Though attending members are very often competitors, your roundtable represents one of the few times that they may gather in a non-competitive, informal environment to discuss mutual threats, opportunities, issues, and solutions. For this reason, roundtables are viewed by most participants as invaluable, productive, and revitalizing.

Your roundtable satisfies their need to associate with a knowledgeable peer group and to indulge in a topic they know and live. Your role, as the facilitator, gives you instant credibility and permits you to build rapport with your market. The key elements of an effective roundtable are as follows:

- The discussion should focus on a single, pertinent topic, which changes with each roundtable. You must know the market, the topic, and the impact it has on the industry.

- Two or more market centers-of-influence should be in attendance. Centers-of-influence give you and your roundtable credibility and attract other members to the discussion. An excellent method to ensure that centers attend is to invite them to be guest speakers, select the topic, invite other associates, etc.

- Limit the time that you speak to the introduction of the topic and/ or the guest speaker. Your objective is to listen and listen well. The needs of the market will develop as the discussion unfolds.

- You don't have to rent out Madison Square Garden for your roundtable. Keep the group small to facilitate an open discussion; large groups are impersonal and prohibitive. Experience indicates 10-15 participants is an ideal size. A rule of thumb to use in determining the quantity of invitations to send out is a ratio of 4 to 1, e.g. 40 to 60 invitations to net 10-15 participants.

- Always diversify. The targeted participant population should be a mixture of existing clients, key prospects, and other market supporters. Loss control specialists from carriers make excellent guest speakers and attendees.

- Keep the invitations simple (see sample in the Online Library.). Like the pre-approach letter, they should be limited to the date, time, location, topic, etc. All must be personalized and should be mailed one month in advance of the gathering.

- Your guests love to eat, so you may wish to serve a simple lunch or breakfast to provide an additional incentive to attending.

- Follow up each invitation with a phone call to confirm attendance. If unable to confirm, use the phone contact to set up another appointment to service, interview, or present. Never waste a phone contact.

- Schedule two follow-up calls, one two weeks in advance and another two days in advance of the gathering.

- Prior to ending the session, have the group select the topic for the next session and inform them of the date, time, and location of the next gathering.

- Follow up with a letter to each participant (see sample) within one week of the meeting and another to those who could not attend in the same week.

- Once again, be consistent and proactive. Your system must be clear to all involved and your events must be scheduled regularly throughout the year.

Association Memberships

Be a contributing part of a group—it will give you a hefty dose of credibility. Adding your name to the channel market's membership organization as an associate or full member is a logical step toward building credibility, contacts, and opportunities within the market. Your regular affiliation with these groups and your active participation in their interests, issues, and activities establishes you as an industry insider. Initially your role will be that of an active observer, carefully listening for the needs of the association's members while identifying centers-of-influence.

Eventually, your relationship with the group will blossom and your advice, opinion, and participation will be requested. This will happen only if you remain an active member of the association and if you consistently donate your time and energy to their projects. If, on the other hand, you approach the membership with the sole purpose of drumming up business, you will be viewed as a parasite and you will be avoided.

Like everything else that we have reviewed, regular demonstrations of integrity, trust, and value must precede the development of real opportunity. It is not uncommon for associations to be approached by eager producers looking to market a discounted specialty program to the members. From the beginning, you must make them aware of just how different you are. Eventually, you may wish to design a hybrid product for the group, but not until you know the issues, the players, and you have earned their trust. The following is a suggested plan of action:

- Create a list of all market-related trade associations; include those of major suppliers and other potential market influences and affiliates. Association lists, addresses, phone numbers, and contact persons can be found on the internet. If you are marketing to a diverse population in a defined geographic nest, your target associations will include chambers of commerce, rotary clubs, and civic organizations.

- Contact each with an adapted pre-approach letter. Request information on membership demographics, guidelines, dues, association publications, meeting schedules, etc.

- Review your list with existing centers-of-influence and other market contacts to determine which associations are most popular and credible. Select three target associations based upon your research and request a referral or introduction from existing client members or centers-of-influence to the appropriate contact within the organization.

- Contact the presidents of each association and inform them of your experience in the market and of your desire to affiliate with the organization. Probe for specific association or member needs. Request newsletter publication information and possible topics of interest.

- Having determined the needs of the association and its membership, re-establish your contact and review what direction your involvement with the association can take. Options will include writing for the newsletter or trade journal, hosting seminars, giving speeches, etc. Also request a copy of the membership roster.

- Join the association and stay in contact with the group's decision-makers by attending all association meetings and hosting your own business and social functions regularly.

- Service the association as you would service your best client, regardless of the initial return on your investment. Your success will evolve from your determination and persistence to make the association better for having met you. This must be your objective.

Networking

James F. Lewin, a former executive at Security Pacific National Bank, once said that "activity is the life blood of a successful selling process. Networking is probably the most effective way of creating activity". An appropriate line. We can all agree that some of your best prospects may never actually buy insurance from you. However, if you build the relationship correctly, they can and will lead you to others within the market that need your help, usually people with an immediate and well-defined requirement who under normal circumstances may have proven illusive. Additionally, other vendors and industry observers may be aware of whom best in the market to approach and when it is a good time to do so. Chief among this group and perhaps the most influential are the financial advisors—bankers, CPAs, lawyers, brokers, etc. These professionals, in one capacity or another, impact every investment decision made by their clients and they are often the first to become aware of a developing need within the market. I strongly recommend that you take the time and the initiative to build a relationship with this secondary market. To approach this targeted group, employ the same strategy we outlined in the preceding section on association membership.

Once again, you must clearly communicate your ability to help their clients. Workshops are a very effective method to attract the attention of these specialists. For instance, an EPLI program for attorneys or a session on alternative markets for CPAs will draw the crowd that you are looking for. It doesn't hurt to be in a position to trade referrals with the right circle of friends.

Articles for Publication

Here's a choice. You can dazzle a dinner party with your thoughts on banks merging with agencies or you can put those thoughts down on paper, have it published in American Banker, be read by 250,000 readers, get extra copies and send them out to prospects. Voila, you're immortalized as a credible source on the topic. The credibility and exposure that is created by having an article appear in a trade journal, newspaper, or in an association newsletter is tremendous. "Getting Published" is relatively easy, providing that you have something of value to offer that is timely, well written, and meets with the specifications of the publisher. These will vary depending on the nature of the publication and its purpose. Presenting your article for publication is best done systematically. Here are the steps to follow:

- Set a quarterly goal for article submissions and use a goal planning sheet to help you stay on track.
- From your research and market surveys, develop three or four risk management topics that are pertinent to your market. New twists on old topics are good; new strategies that address new issues are better. Your selected topics need not be directly insurance related, however. You may wish to submit an article that profiles an industry member, an existing client, or a center-of-influence.

- Create a prospect list of all publications you desire to approach and request from each their publishing guidelines. Inform them of your desire to submit an article for publication and review with them the proposed topic or topics that you intend to write about. Ask the publisher for his or her thoughts and assistance to design the article to match the format of the magazine. Request specific information on desired article length, measured in number of words.

- On the basis of this information and your market research, write your article and run it past a few "critics" prior to submitting it. It should be submitted in its final form—most editors prefer not to edit. And they hate to rewrite.

- After a peer or client review, submit the article to the targeted publications, one at a time. Include a cover letter that briefly summarizes the topic and the impact to the market. Specifically answer the question, "Why would somebody want to read it?"

- Follow up each submission with a phone call. Be willing to re-submit the "draft" after making any suggested changes and be sure to indicate that you are not requesting any compensation. Even so, you could very well be paid anyway.

- You might be requested to send a picture of yourself that will be published with the article. If you are serious about regularly publishing articles, get your press shot done in advance of your submission. Use only a studio shot. Portrait shops know how to shoot these press shots and they offer them very economically. Do not try this at home. Also, be prepared to "Zip" (a compression procedure) your photo to the magazine via e-mail. Most production editors prefer online photos, 300 dpi or higher (called "full resolution" in publishing circles), and in the TIFF (.tif) format. Avoid the JPEG (.jpg) format. Color is always preferable to black-and-white.

- Continue this process with each article written and with every publication that you have targeted. When you are published, request copies from the magazine to use as a future mailing. You will have to pay a nominal amount for these magazine quality copies; however, they are dramatically better than photocopies. If a customer's decision comes down to the industry expert whose face appeared in the business section of the local newspaper or the insurance professional without the photo and the byline, the "expert" wins most every time.

Centers-of-Influence

Centers-of-influence are the decision-makers for the industry. They are also the community leaders, elected officials, and board members. Their buying habits, strategies, programs, and policies are closely monitored and usually mimicked by others within the channel market or the community. A simple nod of approval from a center-of-influence is an instant credibility maker, to say nothing of what a referral from them can do.

Your objective in approaching a center-of-influence should only be to establish a relationship and to learn more about the market. Any attempt to "sell" to the center will result in an abrupt dismissal. You will fall into the same pit of rejection that houses those that have preceded you with the same failed approach. Please understand, eager producers looking for the "one big hit" are constantly barraging centers-of-influence. They will not waste time with any of them or with you if they feel at all cajoled. In order to be perceived as different, you must be different. This requires a polished, professional, and practiced approach, as follows:

- From your research, identify the centers-of-influence in your market or geographic nest. List all known affiliations, associations, and potential referral sources. The best way to meet a center-of-influence is to be introduced by a friend in common.

- Contact each center-of-influence to request an informal meeting. Make an extra effort to let him or her know that the meeting is only for an interview and that you are not attempting to sell anything. Indicate your desire to learn as much about the target market as possible so that you may service it effectively. Mention that you consider them to be highly informed and extremely influential within the industry and, as such, an excellent resource for the information that you need. Follow up every contact, including this initial one, with a thank you letter.

- Offer to meet with the center on his or her terms, wherever and whenever they wish. You must be extremely flexible.

- Develop a questionnaire to use at the interview that will keep the conversation focused. Plan to review your existing approaches to the market and invite any new ideas on different approaches. Probe for specific needs and, if appropriate, ask the center for an interview or to speak on a particular topic at a roundtable or other client gathering.

- Do not ask for referrals at this early stage in the relationship; however, certainly accept them if they come. You can ask for a recommendation to others that can assist in a further evaluation of your ideas or add further insight. These referrals will usually be to other centers-of-influence.

- Whether an appointment is made or not, design a system that will ensure that you are making contact with each center monthly. Your system may include updates on your progress, newsletters, invitations to roundtables and focus groups, handwritten notes, phone calls, etc. Staying consistently visible and viable at all levels of the market is critical.

- Remember; send a thank you note after every contact. Some might call it "killing them with kindness" but it will be appreciated—and remembered.

Focus Groups

Similar to a roundtable, the concept behind a focus group is to bring together members of a market to share their experience and develop solutions to industry-related risk management and loss-control issues. A focus group differs from a roundtable discussion in structure and facilitation.

Typically, a focus group keys in on one or two specific items at a session that are chosen in advance by all participants. The group is usually made up of high-level decision-makers and centers-of-influence and the meetings generally run longer than a roundtable discussion. It is generally a good idea to limit the size of the group to 10 participants.

Facilitate the session at an aesthetically pleasing location that is free from interruptions, like a hotel conference room or a restaurant's banquet area, which is usually set aside from the main dining room (but close enough to the food). Topic selection is made by the group with the objective of problem solving. As with the roundtables, your role is to facilitate and provide a forum for discussion, nothing more. Follow the same guidelines listed under "Roundtables" to design your system, with the following exceptions:

- Participants should be limited to decision-makers and centers-of-influence. This protects the integrity of the discussion.

- Focus group meetings should be scheduled well in advance and held consistently throughout the year. A once-per-quarter format is the most popular.

- Membership in a high-level industry focus group is both an honor and a privilege. Members who do not clearly see a value in participating or are unwilling to commit to attending all scheduled sessions should not be invited.

- Make it nice. Your short-term investment in making the setting relaxing, luxurious, and completely compatible will make the experience pleasurable for everyone and keep them coming back.

- Consider hosting the focus group at a country club or retreat center. This will enable you to combine your formal session with some informal recreation. Participants will usually pay for the privilege and certainly welcome the release.

Seminars and Workshops

More teaching-oriented than roundtables or focus groups, seminars and workshops are ideal presentation formats to use when the market needs to be educated. They are also used to efficiently showcase a new product or service to a large segment of the market. Though interactive, the intent of these sessions is to disseminate new information and they must be formally facilitated. The idea is to educate participants by leading them down an information path that leads to you as the solution to the problem. The key is to keep it useful. As simple as it may sound, the greatest danger in hosting a seminar or workshop is not having anything worthwhile to present.

The topic must provide a solution to a need and the benefits of attending must be clearly apparent and lasting. Stick to new and evolving risk management/loss control issues and solutions. Your goal is to provide value for the time spent, not to entertain or socialize. Your credibility and value to the market will correlate with the caliber of the presentation. You may wish to use a guest speaker or professional workshop facilitator to present the information. Loss control specialists, underwriters, claims attorneys, OSHA officials, and other industry experts will line up to assist you, usually at little or no cost. The following steps will assist you in planning for a successful seminar or workshop.

- When selecting your topic, clearly identify what needs will be satisfied by the information that you intend to present. Make a list of these benefits and ensure that they are numerous and tangible. What impact will your presentation have on the market and how will that impact be measured?

- Consider letting your audience pick the topic for you (or carry an idea over from a recent focus group or roundtable). Send out a survey with a list of potential topics along with a cover letter detailing your objective (see sample in the Online Library.). Not only will you get a response that will help to ensure a popular topic; you will also generate a lot of preliminary interest.

- Remember that your workshop or seminar is not a sales presentation. Your goal is to inform and serve the market.

- Review your ideas with selected members of the market and centers-of-influence. Gauge their level of interest by asking them if they will attend. If they hesitate or balk, your topic is not pertinent or the benefits have not been clearly communicated.

- Keep the presentation to a maximum of 3-4 hours with breaks scheduled on the hour. Most workshops and seminars are best scheduled in the morning.

- Unlike roundtables and focus groups, you will want to have as large an audience as possible. Establish a prospect list of potential participants from your existing client base, prospect lists, and other industry providers, making sure that each will benefit from attending. Set an enrollment objective and use a goal planning sheet.

- Do not proceed unless your prospect list numbers at least 60 potential participants.

- Establish the location, time, and agenda two to three months in advance. If guest speakers are to be used, make sure that they participate in this phase of planning.

- Send out invitations to all prospective participants two months in advance. Your invitations should be personalized, identify the need, highlight your solution, and summarize the benefits to be derived from attending.

- Send out personalized enrollment forms two weeks later. Follow up each with a phone call to ensure that the mailings have been received. Use the call to answer any questions and to gauge attendance. Divide your responses into three categories—"Yes," "No," and "Undecided". Next to each no, make a notation of why. If there are too many "no interest" notations, revisit the topic. If you are unable to confirm a minimum of 30 participants, cancel or postpone the event.

- Send additional notifications and enrollment forms one month and two weeks prior to the event. Follow both mailings up with a phone call to confirm attendance. Once again, if the number of confirmed participants falls below 30, cancel the event.

- Call all confirmed and undecided prospects two days in advance of the event to finalize your list of participants.

- Prepare a participant list to hand out at the event; your clients will want to know with whom they are associating. Personalize as much of your presentation material as possible, particularly the handouts or workbooks. Nametags are requisite.

- Prepare an evaluation form to be collected at the end of the presentation. These will be used to measure your impact and identify follow-up opportunities and future topics.

- Following the event, send a personalized letter to each participant (see sample) within one week of the meeting and another to those who could not attend or no-showed in the same week.

Speeches

Just as a seminar or workshop can solidify your reputation as an industry expert with potential customers, so too can a speech. Any opportunity to address an association or a gathering of your market provides additional exposure and further establishes you as the industry insurance specialist. Good speakers with insightful information are always in demand and welcomed additions to conventions, dinners, seminars, etc. The fact that you come free of charge provides an added incentive for your market to utilize your talents. However, in order to take advantage of these opportunities, you must have something of value to offer and you must be a polished presenter.

Regardless of the message, your audience will focus on you, the messenger, first and foremost. Do not enter this arena unless you are confident in your public speaking abilities. This is not a safe testing ground. To receive an unbiased opinion about your skill as a presenter, ask those that have witnessed you in action before and demand an honest evaluation. If the reviews are unfavorable or neutral, try something else. If you are confident in your ability to address an audience, the following suggestions will improve your opportunities to do so.

- From your research on the market, develop a prospect list of association conventions, trade shows, and other industry gatherings. If you are already an active member in one or more of these groups, start with the home team.

Almost every marketing technique that we have reviewed requires a prospect list of one form or another. We strongly encourage you to invest in contact management software.

- You should be aware of who among your existing clients is active in these associations, if any. A referral to the speaker selection committee is better than a cold introduction. If you do not have a home team or you cannot find a referral source, please continue to the next step.
- Create a pre-approach letter that identifies you as a potential speaker, your area of expertise, your message, and why it is pertinent.
- Identify the event planner or decision-maker and send out your letters. Follow up each letter with a phone call, probing for needs and desired topics.
- Follow up each call with a letter that summarizes the discussion and indicates your ability to offer a valuable presentation where appropriate. Enclose a copy of past speeches and a list of your references.
- Speeches are not sales presentations. If perceived as such, you will immediately offend your audience and your host.
- You may wish to record your speech on a CD, audio tape, or videotape. Ensure that you request permission from your host prior to doing so and be willing to make copies available to your audience. At a minimum, prepare a text copy of your speech.
- Request in advance, a list of participants for follow-up and to better qualify your comments.
- Visit the hall or venue you are speaking at least an hour before your presentation. Step up to the podium and get a feel for the room.

Talk to the person who will introduce you, if possible. Rehearse your speech at that time as well.

- That old saw about envisioning the audience in their underwear? Forget it. Instead, rehearse your speech and know your subject cold. Preparation is critical in the speechmaking game.

Client clipping files

Producers are constantly looking for easy and efficient ways to stay in front of prospects and clients. A simple way to do so is the client clipping file. Your clipping file is used to collect information on the market and its members, personalize it, and disperse it when appropriate. Contained within your clipping file are articles on the industry, trends within the market, organizational and personal announcements, etc.

If your market is geographically nested, screen the local newspapers that usually contain significant announcements such as promotions, births, deaths, weddings, contract signings, expansions, court rulings, etc. Once collected, send an appropriate note or card with the original article or announcement whenever possible. You should also consider internet articles as a source of pertinent information regarding your market. Forwarding timely risk management advice, industry information, community news, or simple articles of interest over the Internet tells your clients and potential clients that you are paying attention. It tells them that you are informed, observant, and responsive. You care about what they care about and they know it. Setting up your system involves only a few simple steps, as follows:

- You must, of course, maintain a current list of your clients' and prospects' email addresses. If you haven't been disciplined about getting them, start now. This is a perfect example of why regular check-in calls are so valuable to you and to your clients. Call to update all of your information and to reconnect – especially with your clients who feel orphaned.

- Conduct a search for websites that contain news, stories, and risk management ideas for personal lines. There are more of these sites available than you'll ever have time to review on a regular basis, so pick five or six that you prefer and mark them in your favorites or sign-up for the free newsletter that they almost always offer.

- Conduct an additional search for your community, including local newspapers, local business digests, etc.

- Develop a strategy to consistently review each publication and web site. Team with other producers within your organization who may wish to employ the same strategy.

- Create a designated file to hold all selected clippings. Review the file weekly for time sensitivity and send out pertinent information as appropriate. A word of caution – send only "bits" of information – nothing too long or cumbersome to read – and avoid sending too much too often.

- Do not send jokes, chain letters, cute little quips, or forwarded information from another group or outside source. This stuff is always annoying, sometimes offensive, and may contain a virus.

In addition to your group emails, personal email can and should be used to reach out and connect with clients individually. A sister strategy to the check-in phone call, personal emails are less intrusive and more efficient than calls or face-to-face meetings with your clients. This is not to suggest that email communication should be used to the exclusion of the face-to-face meeting or the proactive call. It is used for those clients that prefer a less intimate contact and to augment your other client communication initiatives.

The list of approaches that we have suggested should not be viewed as all-inclusive. Our goal has been to help you get started on developing an organized, process-driven, personalized marketing program that utilizes new and creative methods to approach, inform, and serve a channel market. It is, however, only a start.

Like the seed analogy I used earlier in the chapter, effective marketing programs take months to hit their rhythm and channel markets take years to develop. Keep that in mind and give your ideas the patience and discipline that they deserve so that you reap the benefits that you deserve. At the very least, recognize the difference between traditional marketing practices and those that allow you to differentiate with integrity. You, your agency, its clients, and our industry must improve insurance selling and buying practices and make room for distinctive new levels of value, integrity, and trust.

A final reminder—we at Polestar maintain a growing online library of sample letters, marketing ideas, marketing program outlines, etc. These can all be found and used by accessing our website at www.gopolestar.com and then clicking on the "Online Library" button.

Chapter Seven:

Differentiating With Integrity

— The Needs Assessment

"In this life we get only those things for which we hunt, for which we strive, and for which we are willing to sacrifice. It is better to aim for something that you want—even though you miss it—than to get something that you didn't aim to get, and which you don't want! If we look long enough for what we want in life we are almost sure to find it, no matter what that objective may be."
— George Matthew Adams

The good news is that the business is out there. Every minute of every day, somebody, somewhere, is faced with the grueling decision of how to best insure their company. The bad news is that many will not be entirely sure of what they are buying, not completely trust who they are buying it from, and sense that "something" is missing from the process. After the transaction, many will be disappointed by reactive and random servicing of their account, feel ignored by their broker, and appropriately question the integrity of their insurance program.

The strategy that I am about to describe will eliminate these anxieties and negative emotions at the start of the relationship by providing what's missing. Knowing that traditional insurance selling behaviors often lack the integrity, value, and trust necessary to build client confidence and create durable client relationships, a pre-sale needs assessment helps clients develop a clearer understanding of overall business risks that can be positively impacted by improved risk management and human resources strategies.

The value-added service planning begins by conducting a needs assessment with the client during the "discovery" phase of the sale. The assumption we are making is that your target marketing program has worked. You have attracted a client and you have successfully differentiated yourself from your competitors. You are about to schedule your first visit to the prospective client's office and it's here that you will begin to demonstrate just how unique you are.

The client is bracing himself, nervously expecting a full bore avalanche of product books, carrier contracts, client lists, and program announcements. He is expecting that you will request a copy of all current polices, current bid specifications, and five years of loss-runs. He is expecting you to meet with a small executive team, headed by the CFO, to review just enough additional information to allow you formulate a competitive bid. Finally, he is expecting you to push for a close and to wrap the deal up in as little time as possible.

> *You, of course, will do nothing of the kind.*

Instead, right off the bat you are going to stake out the high ground. How so? By patiently doing the footwork necessary for truly getting to know your client while at the same time allowing your client to get to know you. You are courting your client, easing your way into the relationship rather than trying to sell or bargain your way in.

Enter the needs assessment, a simple and easy-to-execute preliminary step in the sales process that will allow you to determine each client's corporate culture, composition, and risks. The results of the assessment will allow you to reach beyond the normal process of reviewing existing coverage and rates by obtaining a clear sense of each client's operations, convictions, and specific needs. This enlightenment will enable you to specifically tailor programs and strategies designed to proactively protect company assets, prevent injuries, and ultimately reduce the cost of insurance. That satisfies the primary interests of the business owner—value and budget.

Of course, not everyone has the same wants and needs. Your needs assessment should be designed to be user-friendly enough for potential clients at all levels in the market and some form of needs assessment is appropriate for every account—including personal lines, BOPs, and small middle market companies. Usually, the larger the account, the more the exposure to risk, and the more complex the needs assessment becomes.

Scott Addis, president and founder of The Addis Group, is an industry leader in the design and use of risk management/needs assessment tools. Convinced that his agency could "grow and prosper without sales people, that expanded risk management resources could be the ultimate sales tool that would cement the agent/client relationship"*, Scott has tracked his agency's performance and compared their results against traditional industry benchmarks. He reports* the following:

- Exceptional client acquisition ratios; hit ratios are in excess of 80% compared to the industry average of 10-15%.

- Explosive and efficient growth of new business commissions.

- The Agency is perceived to be a trusted colleague rather than an insurance supermarket. This status occurs as a result of the in-depth analysis of the insured's operations, facilities, exposures, and risk management standards.

- There is no competition from competing brokers during the assessment process. The incumbent agent or broker is typically not a factor.

- The assessment enhances the insured's ability to focus on risk management issues rather than on insurance products and price.

- The assessment process creates strong, long-term client relationships that evolve from employee, supervisor, and management interviews.

- Insurance companies respect the comprehensive nature of the assessment. It permits the carriers to price an account more aggressively, expand coverage, and streamline claims/risk control services as their fixed costs are reduced and underwriting results enhanced.

- As a percentage, fewer clients will choose to bid out the insurance placements.

- Client satisfaction, as measured by the number of referrals received from clients and centers-of-influence, is dramatically increased.

- The differentiated consultative approach is marketable to trade associations and can be tailored to specific industry groups.

---

* *"Rough Notes"* Magazine, August 1999

- The comprehensive nature of the assessment positions the producer to expand the business relationship into other income-generating areas including employee benefits, financial services, and personal insurance.
- Client retention rates exceed 90%.

Benefits experienced by the Insured include:

- The needs assessment provides a tool through which the insured can assess the degree to which its risk management policies, procedures, and controls adequately respond to the firm's exposures and assets at risk.
- Because the assessment is performed away from the insurance "bidding process", the insured is fully focused on critical risk management issues. These include loss prevention orientation and training, safety committee functions, substance abuse, employment practices, accident investigation, emergency preparedness, and claims management.
- Action plans are developed to address issues arising out of the risk management assessment process. The plans allow the insured to proactively participate in a formal risk avoidance program.
- Claims frequency and severity are reduced along with insurance costs. The process gives insurance carriers confidence in reducing premiums as their underwriting results are improved and fixed costs reduced.
- The information gives the insured the ability to negotiate expanded insurance coverage terms and conditions.
- The client has the opportunity to observe the professionalism and measure the results of the producer before making an insurance placement decision.

Benefits experienced by the Carriers include:

- Underwriting results are improved as the needs assessment has identified and addressed critical risk factors.
- The underwriters have comfort in aggressively pricing the risk.
- Fixed/operating costs are significantly reduced in three key areas: underwriting, risk control, and claims.

- Retention of business is increased as interactive, long-term relationships are developed with the insured. The insured learns to place more emphasis on the carrier's value-added resources and expertise than on the price of the product.
- The assessment pinpoints issues that need attention and provides an action plan for completion.
- The carrier works hand-in-hand with the producer as a member of the insured's risk management team. The carrier has great visibility in the eyes of the insured.
- The carrier gains comfort to consider broadening coverage and expanding limits if the audit confirms the insured's risk management practices meet or exceed standards.

Your needs assessment can and will provide you with similar benefits providing that you develop it, use it, and trust it. Notice that every benefit derived from the assessment enhances one or more of the following objectives:

1. Improved Production
2. Improved Account Performance and Profitability
3. Improved Client Retention
4. Improved Efficiency.

These are good objectives to target because they are the cornerstones on which your professional success will rest.

Introducing the needs assessment

Generally, a needs assessment is created for each new prospect and is presented to the potential client as the first and most important step in your insurance program development process. At the very onset of your discussions, at the early introduction phase of your budding relationship, your potential client learns that you are interested in custom-developing an insurance program and that you are not intending to simply shop and hawk an existing policy for a better price.

Based on the time it might take to do a thorough needs assessment and present your findings and recommendations, this strategy also encourages you and the prospect to initiate your discussions well in advance of the normal harvesting season—allowing you to gain access to the account and demonstrate your ability long before your competitors have even considered picking up the phone.

Be prepared. Prior to your arrival, the client should be briefed on what the objectives of the meeting are. While setting up this appointment, inform the client that the appointment will be used to gather some preliminary information that's needed for you to conduct a more thorough analysis of the organization, its culture, its people, and its insurance program. Be matter of fact about it and let them know your chief responsibility is to be a good listener. I often say to the client "I'll only be bringing a sharp pencil, a new legal pad, lots of questions, and a clean set of ears". I make it clear that this is not a sales call or a product pitch. At this point, you may describe the process that you are about to walk the client through and offer to send along an advanced copy of your outline.

Of course, it will help if you know what the process is and if you have an outline to send ... so, on to the next step.

Creating the needs assessment:

The needs assessment is nothing more than a series of questions that you and/or other members of your team (if available) will ask about the client company that you are interviewing. The questions should be designed to provide you with a comprehensive analysis of the client's corporate philosophy, structure, and exposures. The answers to these questions will allow you to look beyond the issues of policy and rates by gaining a true understanding of your client's organizational culture and specific needs. Although your underwriter will favor any submission that includes this type of cultural assessment, these questions are not underwriting questions. They are intended to provide you with insight that will enable you to specifically tailor programs, services, and strategies designed to protect assets, reduce insurance costs, and bring tangible value to the relationship.

The types of questions and the number of them that you ask depend entirely on you and the nature of the client that you are interviewing. For instance, size does matter—in the insurance business, anyway. Generally, the larger clients tend to have more complex insurance programs and require more questions to completely identify the needs and expectations. Be careful, however, more is sometimes less and a few carefully targeted questions may be enough to give you most of what you need to build your plan. You will have ample opportunity to fill in any gaps as your relationship evolves.

Here are some areas to consider investigating when building a needs assessment. The lists of categories are by no means all-inclusive nor are they all necessary to cover with every account. Draw from your own expertise to formulate your questions and use them as a springboard to educate your prospect, define your involvement, and build the insurance program.

Potential Categories for Property and Casualty Needs Assessment Questions:

Relationship with Agent	Business Recovery
Relationship with Carrier	Data Storage/Security
Buying Practices	Employee Benefits
Knowledge of existing program	Motor Vehicle Safety
Industry & Community Involvement	Retirement Plans/Fiduciary
Alternative Markets	Employee Wellness
Business Practices	Substance Abuse
Company Structure	OSHA Compliance
Cultural Assessment	Policy Review
The Insurance Market Place	Reserve Analysis
Insurance Buying Practices	Fleet Safety
Employment Practices	Safety Committee
Claims Management	Perpetuation Plans
Loss Control Programs	Expansion/Contraction Plans
Orientation & Training	Employee Development Programs
Environmental Issues	Customer Profile
General Liability Issues	Service Standards
Endorsements	Safety Incentive Programs
Disaster Planning	

Potential Categories for Personal Lines Needs Assessment Questions:

Frequency of Agent contact	Rental Property
Home safety awareness	Mold
Home Protective Devices	Earthquake, Flood
Insurance Buying Practices	Pets
Knowledge of coverage	Replacement Cost Estimates
Knowledge of limits	Mortgage Protection
Loss-free Discounts	Retirement Planning
Computer Coverage	Greenery Coverage & Debris Removal
Credit Scoring	Personal Property Endorsements
Home Business	Companion Credits
Watercraft	Complete Auto Policy Review

Environmental Issues	Personal Auto Discounts
Personal Liability Issues	Driver Training Credits
Payment Plans	Seasonal Use of Vehicles
Emergency Planning	Audio & Visual Equipment
Additions and Alterations	Lease Coverage
Wills	Rental Coverage
Life Insurance	Safe Driver Programs
Service Expectations	Seminars & Safety Program
Environmental Issues	UM & UIM Coverage

Potential Categories for Employee Benefits Needs Assessment Questions:

Relationship with Agent	Section 125 Plans
Relationship with Carrier	Childcare Programs
Knowledge of existing program	Supplemental Plans
Industry & Community Involvement	Payroll Deduction
Business Practices	Vision Plans
Company Structure	Tuition Reimbursement
Cultural Assessment	Long-term Care
The Insurance Market Place	Prescription Plans
Insurance Buying Practices	Retirement Plans
Employment Practices	Company/Employee Contributions
Managed Care Options	Employee Wellness Programs
Voluntary Programs	Managed Care Options
Flex Spending Accounts	Substance Abuse Programs
Dental Plans	Life Insurance Plans
COBRA	Bonus/Incentive Programs
Disability Program	Employee Compensation
Employee Advisory Committee	Claims Management

In our Online Library (accessed through www.gopolestar.com) you'll find sample needs assessments that contain questions created from these categories. There is a simple assessment for personal lines, a comprehensive assessment for a large commercial account, an underwriter's assessment for determining the needs and goals of an agent or broker, and a benefits assessment for small cases. You may print them and use them as they are or you may use them as a guide to creating your own. As you read them, keep in mind that the traditional underwriting questions have already been addressed and that the answers to these inquires will provide the information that is needed to create a customized value-added service plan that:

1. Establishes tangible performance benchmarks for you and for the client.
2. Proactively schedules and defines your service activities.
3. Differentiates you from your competitors.
4. Enlightens the carrier to the culture of the client and improves marketability of the account.
5. Gives the client a demonstration of your expertise, integrity, and ability to proactively build a partnership.
6. Has an impact—it will reduce the frequency and severity of claims.

To develop your own needs assessments for personal lines, benefits, life, surety, small commercial, middle market, and large commercial accounts, I suggest that you build an inventory of questions for each pertinent category (shown above) and, based on the size and complexity of the account, select the appropriate number of questions to include from each category. Please remember that these are only sample questions. Make your list of questions as extensive or as abbreviated as you deem necessary and add or delete categories as needed. If you are uncomfortable about a specific topic or a series of questions, bring along an expert. Many carriers will be more than happy to send a representative and some will let you borrow a loss control specialist for your appointment.

Conducting the needs assessment:

As I have mentioned previously, the larger the account, the larger the needs assessment and the more time it will take to complete it. Be thorough and take your time to get the client's current program and future needs right. I encourage the interviewing of other employees within the organization so that you gather a healthy sampling of perspectives and experiences. You may wish to sit in on a safety committee meeting, visit each location in a multiple location organization, and work with a pre-selected carrier to properly study the nuances of the account and conduct a comprehensive loss-control analysis. You will certainly want to educate the client throughout the process by explaining various coverage options and the pros and cons of each, updating them on our industry and our market place, introducing risk management and loss control suggestions, and so on. Upon completion of the needs assessment, you will want to summarize and present your findings (good and bad) and provide an itemized list of suggested corrections and enhancements to their current insurance program. In short, the more thorough and formal you are with your assessment, the deeper you drill down into the organization, the more information you get and the more customized and valuable their program becomes.

Time is the issue—the time it takes to do this right and to do this well, time that is not available during the normal hunting and buying season (90 days or less before expiration). Sure, you can try to rush through it and pull something together in time to submit a bid, but the value of the process will get lost in the shuffle, the information that you gather will be cursory, the prospect will probably find you more annoying than helpful, and you will not differentiate yourself as a value-added provider because you will have had no time to demonstrate your capability. It will look like what it is—a selling tactic. That's the last thing the client wants.

Instead, do it right. This assessment is best done mid-term or earlier when the prospect is not trying to balance the inquires of a number of competing producers while worrying about an impending expiration date. Present it for what it is—an in-depth, cost-free analysis of their entire insurance program, complete with expert ideas and unbiased suggestions. The prospect should quickly grasp the significance of what is being offered, see the value in participating, and willingly engage in the process long before he or she normally starts thinking about the renewal. When this happens, you're in. Better yet, you're in for the right reasons. When it doesn't happen, you are competing against traditional insurance buying practices and it may take a year or more to fully evolve the buyer. If you feel that the account is worthy, it is worth the wait.

A word on smaller accounts. Admittedly, smaller accounts and personal lines prospects do not necessitate an extensive assessment and therefore will not require a great deal of time to implement the strategy and summarize the results. Timing, then, is much more discretionary.

Once the decision is made to move ahead with the assessment, the implementation steps are as follows:

Step 1 – Assessment Orientation

Rather than rush right into the assessment questions (which can feel like a bright-light interrogation to the client), it is advisable to conduct a preliminary meeting with the decision maker(s) and key staff members so that you may define the objectives of the investigation and describe what and who will be involved in the process. Large, comprehensive assessments may involve a number of interviews and visits by an assessment team and therefore require an established timeline and a disciplined approach. I suggest that you use an action plan to map out the roles and the goals of each participant in the process to help ensure proper coordination. A sample action plan is available in the Online Library (www.gopolestar.com). Please note the account-specific comments and observations noted throughout the action plan and on the final two pages. Sharing this information with the team helps to avoid uncomfortable moments during the process.

What if I don't have a team? Great question—not everyone has those kinds of resources. But if you are going to commit to doing business this way, try working with a few carriers that see the value in partnering with you and are willing to commit the time and resources necessary to help you with the assessment when you need it. This, of course, requires you to pre-select the carrier and make an early commitment; however, the benefits of doing so far out-weigh the risk of making a "wrong" selection.

Good underwriters will help you to a degree; great underwriters will support you however they can; and a true partnering underwriter will prioritize your submission, defend a referral when needed, and round out your relationship with the prospective client. It's all good and everybody wins.

Step 2 – Implementing the needs assessment

Larger accounts require a carefully coordinated implementation plan that usually involves a series of meetings and a number of people on both ends, while smaller accounts can be assessed without a lot of formality. Still, the assessment should be conducted as a separate and distinct step in the development of a customized insurance program.

Rather than lumping it in with all of the other activities associated with quoting a new account (current policy review, loss review, etc.), it is highly recommended that the assessment be conducted during a separate meeting with the client and that it be the only agenda item for that meeting. This helps to ensure that the assessment is taken seriously and given the weight that it deserves. Additionally, this is the point in the sales process that you gain a distinct advantage over your competing agents—it should be highlighted and not camouflaged by other routine account development activities.

To be effective, you will need the full attention and cooperation of those participating in the assessment. It is best conducted in a relaxed environment where the participants can be protected against ringing phones, in-boxes, to do lists, knocks on the doors, and other interruptions. If available, a conference room seems to work best. If a "neutral" space is not available, consider taking the prospect to breakfast or lunch or meeting in your office. For the client it's a "paperless" visit. Since most of the information that you need is in their head (thoughts, opinions, goals, etc.), there is no need for them to lug a briefcase overstuffed with their policies, "files", and documentation. Reassure the prospect that you will review all of the above at a later date.

Clients may feel they're entering uncharted territories here. Being unfamiliar with this level of due-diligence, it is quite natural for any participant in the assessment to be a little defensive and guarded. Ease them into the process by reviewing your objective and the intent of the assessment—you are there to help, not to pass judgement.

The assessment is a tool that provides you with the information that you need to make sure that you can design a program that provides what they need. You are not interrogating; you are learning. Remind them that your objective is only to provide them with enough information to make an educated decision about their insurance program, it is not to sell them a cookie-cutter policy. Essentially what you're doing is talking about your client's business. Who hasn't met an entrepreneur or business owner who doesn't like talking about their business?

To further ease any client anxieties, bring a standard "confidentiality" agreement with you and sign it for the prospect. Much of the information that you are asking for might be "sensitive" and it is critically important that the prospect can trust you. As the relationship blossoms, they will of course come to trust and respect your integrity. However, at this stage in the relationship, it is best to provide a hedge against any doubt. Besides, it's an effective way to convey to the client that you're on his "team".

Summarizing your findings

Upon the completion of the assessment, it's showtime. Call together all members of the assessment team along with the decision makers for the prospective company (or family). At this meeting, you will present the following:

1. An overview of the assessment process—who met with whom, when and where.

2. A copy of the assessment tool or questionnaire.

3. A summary of what you discovered—what they were doing well and where you feel they need improvement.

4. Your itemized recommendations and adjustments to their current insurance program along with your reasons for making the recommendations. These include coverage and carrier recommendations.

5. Recommended program objectives for the next policy year and beyond.

6. Finally, and perhaps most important, your schedule of actions, activities, and events that will support the accomplishment of the objectives. ***This becomes your Value-Added Service Plan.***

Preparing to build the Value Added Service Plan

Why do most client service programs fail? As I've said before, it's because they don't effectively define and measure up to the client's service expectations. Most often, this results from never asking and/or assuming client expectations. Big mistake. The message the client absorbs is that we are arrogant. "Imagine", the client thinks, dark clouds forming in his mind, "This clown thinks that he is going to represent me and he doesn't even know me."

Fortunately, the needs assessment allows us to create a much different impression. We diplomatically uncover gaps in coverage, erroneous reserves, and loss control issues without coming off as pushy or critical. The needs assessment allows us to experience and define the culture of the organization and its people. It establishes very specific product and program benchmarks, educates, and most importantly, it allows us to specify the client's service and support expectations. Knowing them in advance rather than discovering them following a service disappointment, enables us to build a plan of action that proactively fulfills them and, in most cases, exceeds them.

Let's assume that you have completed a needs assessment on "Acme Cement Company" shown in the sample action plan in the Online Library. In addition to product, price, carrier, and coverage recommendations, your assessment uncovered the following:

- There is no standing safety committee.

- Back strain "lifting" injuries account for an unusually high percentage of claims.
- Driver safety training is sporadic and not conducted by the incumbent carrier.
- The incumbent agent only visits the home office and only does so at time of renewal. Account administration is handled by internal CSRs that have never visited the client.
- There has been no formal training in the following:
  1. Slip, trip, and fall
  2. Sexual Harassment
  3. Diversity
  4. Crisis Management
  5. Blood-borne Pathogens
  6. Claims Management/Reporting
- There is no posted procedure for emergency medical care.
- There are no formal security programs for visitors.
- Many claims are stale-dated and appear over-reserved.

Based on these findings, the following sample recommendations would be made:

- Establish a formal, employee led safety committee that meets once per month. This will dramatically improve the organization's "safety consciousness" , create an incentive program for accident free workdays, establish formalized risk management training programs and initiatives, and monitor and analyze trends in accidents and accident reporting standards.

Priority Rating – High
Impact Rating – High

- Establish safe lifting standards. Train and reinforce safe lifting techniques and mandate use of loading docks for all deliveries. Consider replacing manual off-loading system with a mechanical

"roller" system or other lifting aid. Deploy loss control engineers to design and monitor a comprehensive program.
Priority Rating – High
Impact Rating – Significant

• Conduct twice-annual driver safety classes for all drivers and invite managers to an accident evaluation seminar in August. Equip all vehicles with accident reporting kits including disposable cameras, reporting guidelines, etc.
Priority Rating – High
Impact Rating – Moderate

• Schedule quarterly account reviews to monitor and assist with the implementation of loss control initiatives, review claims, and conduct site visits. Coordinate these sessions with the account management team and loss control. Attend a minimum of two safety committee meetings annually.
Priority Rating – High
Impact Rating – Moderate

• Conduct documented quarterly risk management and loss control training for all employees. Invite appropriate managers to all agency-sponsored training events. Design customized program templates for implementation and documentation of all workplace safety initiatives.
Priority Rating – High
Impact Rating – High

• Establish, post, and train standardized emergency medical care procedures.
Priority Rating – High
Impact Rating – Moderate

- Develop a standard approach for recording and monitoring all visitors to each location. Create visitor parking areas, sign in/out logs, identification badges, reception area, hardhats, etc.

Priority Rating – High
Impact Rating – Moderate

- Conduct regularly scheduled reserve analysis with underwriters for all reserved claims and adjust as needed.

Priority Rating – High
Impact Rating – High

The "Priority" and "Impact" ratings are assigned based on the significance of the finding and the potential effect that the corrective action will have on the cost of insurance incurred by the client. A typical list of recommendations for a client of this size would usually be more extensive and include lesser priorities as well.

Now it's time to begin sowing the seeds of all your hard work. Having thoroughly reviewed and presented your findings and recommendations with the client, including everything that the team found to be positive and adequate, you now steer the discussion away from the current program by outlining your vision of their future program. At this point the client is convinced that you know the organization and its people better than any producer that has ever come before you. They are impressed by your thoroughness and honored by the time and attention that you have invested in their company. You are clearly different and believably better. They have first hand experience with your professionalism, integrity, and value. They are probably ready to turn over a BOR based on the work that you have already done. Wonderful!

And it's about to get even better.

Chapter Eight:

The Value Added Service Plan

- Bringing It All Together

"To give real service you must add something which
cannot be bought or measured with money, and
that is sincerity and integrity."
— Donald A. Adams

There's no shortage of companies that have earned household names based on their ability to provide service and value to their customers. Consider Federal Express, the parcel delivery giant that was founded on the premise it would "absolutely, positively" get your package to its destination by 10 a.m. the next morning. That service model made history—and billions for the company.

Then there's Ford Motor Co., the firm that founded the customer service model back when the term rarely passed the lips of captains of industry—if they knew it at all. Not Henry Ford. Here's what he had to say about the value of service. "The trouble with a great number of us in the business world is that we are thinking hardest of all about the dollar we want to make. Now that is the wrong idea from the start. I'll tell you the man who has the idea of service in his business will never need to worry about profits."

Of course, titans liked Ford "walked the talk". They made service and value a high priority and prospered. That's one reason why the greatest compliment that I receive from my clients is when I'm told that I "walk my talk". For a client to acknowledge that I do for them what I am asking them to do for their clients means that I don't come to the table empty handed, that I have demonstrated a unique level of personalized service that they value—and appreciate. It also means that we have reached beyond the normal boundaries of a client/producer relationship to form a personal bond that is mutually productive and equally beneficial.

It amazes me how little effort is needed to create and manage these high-level, service-focused client relationships. In fact, I still kick myself for waiting so long to make the break from the traditional service philosophy. Not that I was complacent—far from it. I'd always felt a sincere obligation to take care of my clients and to meet their expectations. But service (particularly personalized and proactive service) was always a struggle. Caught up as I was between a jumble of shifting priorities, crises, and needs, an emphasis on service fell between the cracks. It wasn't long before those cracks grew wider and my business began to suffer.

That was then and this is now. Things began to change as soon as I shifted to the sales, marketing, and priority management systems that are the cornerstones of this book. I became more consistent, more efficient, more productive, and more available. Because I learned to use the same activities to attract and develop a client as I do to service a client, service activities and value-added service plans were integrated with the sales and marketing plans to create one seamless, proactive client management strategy.

Here's what I mean: if I'm hosting a client roundtable or a workshop, I invite prospective clients as well as existing clients. Our electronic newsletter is sent out to both groups and I regularly give out advice and assistance to those who need it and will use it, regardless of whether I close any business. Inevitably, I end up attracting clients who are comfortable with our methodology and recognize its value. I retain them as clients because we consistently deliver the value that attracted them in the first place. It is a superbly efficient and incredibly effective way to do business.

My clients appreciate early demonstrations of value, integrity, and trust followed by a comprehensive plan to deliver even more—what they don't want is a bid, a pitch, a policy, and a phone number. Over the course of time I came to understand why the value approach was so powerful compared to the "pitch and pray" system. Let's examine why my system, and the value-added service plan that we will create for you, works so well.

The Psychology of Service

What's more appealing, price or value? In other words, when you buy something, what do you consider most important, the price that you pay or the value that you receive from the product? How much weight do you give to the reputation and credibility of the seller? Do you evaluate competing products and services on cost alone or is quality a determining factor as well? What about the social implications of your selection—will you compare your purchase to what other people have bought and is the status of your selection a priority to you?

The answers depend on what you are buying. In most cases, the size of the purchase and the complexity of the product or service determine the degree of consideration given to these and other "look and feel" conditions. Smaller, "simple" sales such as pencils, speaker wire, fast food, cab rides, and chewing gum tend more toward the commodity price-driven factors because the decisions are low risk and the differences among competing products are reasonably obscure. Look and feel characteristics do exist; however, they are not given much weight.

On the flip side, larger, complex sales such as cars, computers, ***insurance,*** homes, vacations, weddings, and college educations are nearly always determined by look and feel attributes first, and price second.

Marketing, advertising, and public relations firms have been aware of these consumer-buying patterns since cavemen first grunted "how much?" to the traveling sharp stick salesman. It's no secret that product branding and corporate identity are the most vital components of any strategic marketing program—including yours.

To gain traction in any market that is already occupied, providers of products and services must differentiate their offering based upon look and feel factors and create an exclusive "space" or niche for their offering. That is how they attract and retain a client base—by creating brand loyalty.

When a company fails to differentiate their brand with look and feel, they are almost always slapped with a "copycat" label and are forced into the "low-cost provider" space in the market where price, not perception of value, motivates the buyer. Unable to recognize any significant difference between products, these buyers focus only on price and tend to float from one provider to another in search of financial value. As a market segment, these consumers tend to view products and services as commodities to be bid and bargained for. They are fickle, volatile, transient, and disloyal. As a client base, such consumers are a disaster.

That's why, in nearly every section of this book, I've hammered home the point that this is not a good space to be in if you are a provider of insurance programs. Still, I worry. There are enough of your comrades trapped in conventional insurance agencies to fill a dozen football stadiums. There's also an abundance of companies that still depend upon price rather than value to attract and retain their clients. As Mr. T says, "I pity the fools", because as the market continues to harden and the cost of insurance products rise, insurance buying practices will shift dramatically in favor of proactive, value-driven, risk management rich insurance programs.

Insurance buyers will soon realize that the most effective method for controlling their premium levels is to proactively address and reduce the frequency and severity of their claims. Thus, the end game is clear. Agencies and Carriers that are willing and able to participate and manage these programs will attract and retain clients. Those that can't, won't. Fools indeed.

If you are still hanging onto the fantasy that things will return to the way they were, you have to give it up and face up to the reality of this hard market and make the adjustments required by it. Although there will always be a justifiable price-driven, "insurance is a commodity" buying attitude at the lower end of the market, this space is not large enough to accommodate all of the players that are looking to exploit it.

The survivors in this market segment will be the fast, efficient, technology savvy agencies and carriers that compete on a national level and process, rather than service their clients. These are not traditional agencies or companies either—they do not employ producers or service teams, they run call centers and hire processors. Clearly, they're not interested in the relationship-building, service-and-value model that I'm advocating.

What then will become of the traditional agencies/carriers and the people that work there? Pity them, too. They will be consolidated, merged, acquired, or closed by the industry vanguards that saw the changes coming and did something about it. In pure Darwinian fashion, it will be "survival of the fittest".

Okay, you might be wondering what any of this has to do with service. Remember the Big Mac commercials touting the company's "special sauce"? Our model has one, too. The special sauce is the infusion of principled, proactive service strategies into each element of the program. These collective service strategies define your "value proposition".

Our objective all along has been to help you establish and consistently maintain a unique and highly personalized value proposition in your selected market. Your value proposition creates your space and allows you to effectively differentiate. Your sales, marketing, and referral harvesting plans are all designed to attract qualified clients to your value proposition. Your value-added service plan will be crafted to retain them.

What is value-added service?

Simply stated, value-added service means making a sincere, consistent, and proactive commitment to understand your clients' needs and to meet them as they change. Think about the term "value-added". It tells customers that they can expect the rock-solid basics—good products and services, fair prices, and good customer service—but that's not all it's telling them. Value-added service also means adding additional ingredients to that special sauce we were talking about. It means telling clients you'll do what it takes to keep them happy. That you'll go out of your way to add extra services and attention to the provider/client relationship. It tells them that you are serious about keeping the relationship growing and mutually beneficial.

That's where integrity comes in. To be sincere, your motive must be to build a relationship based upon mutual trust and integrity—a relationship that is not contingent on any particular sales event, now or ever. In a value-added sales environment, relationships occur when individuals and organizations form a cohesive bond and agree to work together toward a common objective.

I'm a big football fan and I marveled at the job the New England Patriots did in winning the Super Bowl. They didn't have the best talent or the highest payroll. In fact, nobody gave them a shot. But the coach sold the team on the goal of winning it all—as long as they all stuck together. That's worth noting, because products and services do not form relationships, people do.

Though products, services, money, and information are exchanged, the exchange is a result of and not a cause for the relationship. The healthier the relationship, the more these exchanges take place and visa versa. If you have followed the steps in this program to this point, and I assume that you have, then you have already created your value-added sales and marketing system.

Think of your business as a pyramid. Your sales and marketing plan are your foundation and your value-added service plan is built on top of it, using the same blueprint, of course. In fact, the proactive service activities that appear on your sales and marketing plans are the same activities that we will use to build your value-added service plan.

Essentially, your sales plan is also your service plan. Your activity is fully integrated, consistent, and productive. You remain uniformly visible and viable both before and after every transaction that takes place during the relationship with the client.

No doubt by now you've noticed that value-added service is much more comprehensive than simply taking care of a client claim or question, chasing a certificate, or checking in at time of renewal. These activities and others like them are considered normal administrative servicing practices—the "basics" or routine things that must be done to keep the policy in place.

Don't miss-read me; good account administration is critically important and you won't get anywhere without it. However, good administration is only doing what you should do and what the client anticipates will be done—by any agent.

When contrasted against a fully integrated value-added service system, we quickly see the difference between reacting to an administrative responsibility and proactively satisfying client needs.

Let's objectively compare the characteristics and perceptions of a traditional sales and service model with our value-added approach to determine which is more effective:

Initial Client Contact	*Traditional Approach*		*Value-Added Approach*	
Producer Motive	✗	to make a sale	✓	to build a relationship
Producer Focus	✗	on the product and the price	✓	on the client and the client's need
Producer Behavior	✗	high pressure	✓	conversational
	✗	rushed/frenzied	✓	patient
	✗	opinionated	✓	consultative
	✗	overbearing	✓	listens, questions
	✗	attempts to close	✓	agreements reached

Post Sale Activity	Traditional Approach	Value-Added Approach
Service Behaviors	✗ Reactive – issues are responded to as they develop, no news from clients is considered good news.	✓ Proactive – client interactions continue. Needs are constantly assessed, anticipated, solicited, and creatively satisfied.
Producer Focus	✗ The relationship is dormant; producer contact is limited to renewal activity, special requests, or problems.	✓ The relationship blossoms, contact is frequent. Client communication and consultation continue.
Producer Behavior	✗ Other sales activity significantly limits producers' available time. They become elusive and pass-off most service requests. New business is generated the old fashioned way.	✓ Producers are accessible and highly visible. They continue to service the relationship and utilize existing clients to attract new business opportunities.
	✗ A client's value is determined by the level of premium paid and by what they can do for the producer in the short-term.	✓ Clients are catered to and invested in. Relationships are established with the intention of creating a long-term partnership.

The Results	Traditional Approach	Value-Added Approach
Client Perceptions:	✗ Buyer's remorse is high. Clients feel cajoled and doubt the decision to enter the relationship.	✓ As the relationship grows, client loyalty deepens. The decision to enter into the partnership is trusted.
	✗ There is no perception of value. The decision to buy was based on price. The decision to renew will also be based on price.	✓ Value far beyond the original need for coverage is clearly apparent and trusted, regardless of price.
	✗ Clients feel abandoned, ignored, patronized, and sold to.	✓ Clients feel spoiled, cared about, listened to, and informed.
	✗ Producers are associated with invoices, claims and additional expenses.	✓ Clients view the producer as an informed and interested business partner and consultant.
	✗ There are few if any opportunities or attempts made to cross-sell, harvest referrals, or differentiate on anything other than price.	✓ Exchanges continue to occur as client needs evolve. Referral business is a normal outgrowth of the relationship.
	✗ Accounts are highly susceptible to internal and external competition. Retention is average, bids are common and renewal times are stressful.	✓ Retention is extremely high. Value, not price is the buying motive. Competitors are rarely received, bids are infrequent, and expiration dates are just another day.

It should be obvious by now, at least I hope it is, that a value-added organization and the producers within that organization have a much easier time building and maintaining mutually beneficial relationships with their clients. Clearly, the sensible producer should seek to emulate the right side of this chart as soon as he or she leaps out of bed in the morning. Unfortunately, common sense is not always common practice.

Though recognition of the benefits associated with providing value-added service is high, consistent practice of these principles remains low due to an industry addiction for instant commission dollars on any investment of time and attention. Under these hard market conditions, however, taking shortcuts and grabbing for quick commissions is nearly impossible. Building value-added relationships takes longer and the payoff isn't a near-term one, it's a long-term one. However, when the payoff does materialize, it is usually here to stay.

As tempting as it may be, you can't leap back and forth between the two philosophies, painstakingly attending to an abundance of shifting priorities while attempting to identify true opportunities. The predictable result is a haphazard, reactionary approach to service that quells the disturbances but camouflages the truly rewarding opportunities. Before long, you lose focus and lapse back into old, failed habits.

We know that won't work. And we're not casting aspersions here, either. Many organizations, producers, and service personnel earnestly attempt to differentiate through service and almost all are truly concerned about the welfare of their clientele. This is not a case of "good versus evil." Most are unsuccessful in their efforts because their approach to service replicates their selling habits—load up with clients, build a cookie-cutter, one-size-fits-all service program, and deal with the problems as they develop. While the intentions may be honorable, they're not very workable. Certainly, they're not proactive.

Those organizations that are successful use a different strategy based on relationship building. First, they recognize that the people, not the product and price, are the most important variables in any sales or service model. It immediately becomes a priority to identify with these people and understand their likes, dislikes, culture, habits, and expectations. When it comes to providing service, experience has taught them that different people have different expectations regarding their relationship with any insurance provider. These organizations recognize that the difference between ordinary service and extraordinary service is simply a matter of clarifying each client's expectations at the beginning of the relationship and proactively integrating them into the development of their insurance programs. The client, not the service department, establishes the service standards, best practices, and performance benchmarks.

Second, successful service providers realize that client expectations are fluid and dynamic, changing as the relationship matures. Consequently, these expectations need to be consistently redefined and discussed. These organizations take nothing for granted, routinely verifying their service assumptions rather than presuming that in the absence of a crisis or an obvious conflict, all is well. As these organizations have done their homework and studied their clients' peccadilloes and preferences, they don't confuse "quiet clients" with satisfied clients. Leaving nothing to chance, these organizations regularly investigate what is working, what isn't, and what can be done better. They start proactive and they stay proactive.

Finally, these organizations acknowledge imperfection. Nobody can do it all and nobody can do it perfectly, right? So they accept the reality of their own limitations and they establish these service parameters early in the relationship with the client. Having identified the client's expectations, these producers and service providers honestly and diplomatically outline their own capabilities and expectations. That alleviates "surprises" and takes the unknown out of the equation early in the relationship, minimizing the potential that either party will be disappointed in the future.

Okay, time out for a disclaimer. A magic pill doesn't exist. In fact, I have never seen an ironclad service plan that successfully anticipates every service issue nor do I believe that such a plan can ever be created. Let's face it; ours is not a perfect world nor will people or circumstances ever be entirely predictable. Even with the best made plans, things can and will go wrong. Unforeseen service gaps will occur, problems will arise, and crises will happen, in spite of your proactive service posture.

Unfair as it may seem , this is a part of doing business and it is a part of life. So, as we develop your value-added service plan, I want you to be realistic with your expectations about what the plan will and will not do. Your plan **will**:

- Enable you to integrate your proactive sales and marketing plans with an equally proactive, custom-developed, needs-based, value-added service strategy.

- Be your blueprint for scheduling consistent value delivery to your key clients over time, ensuring that you are a visible and viable insurance partner.

- Make it possible for you to establish well-defined client service expectations and manage them as they change.

- Provide your clients with an unprecedented level of insurance program management and support.

Your value-added service plan **will not**:

- Be that "magic bullet". Certificates will still get lost, some claims will be denied or delayed, clients will still miss payments, and carriers will miss deadlines. You will still not be able to control the uncontrollable and predict every contingency. However, you will be able to better influence those around you to become more responsive and work more proactively. Things will never be perfect but they will be consistently better.

- Meet every client expectation. Despite your efficiency and effectiveness, you will never be able to be all things to everybody— nor should you desire to be. You will always have limitations on your available time and resources. Limitations, however, do not have to lead to client disappointments if they are communicated up front.

- Remain etched in stone. Circumstances change for you and for the client on a regular basis. As is the case with all of our plans, your value-added service plan will undergo regular revisions.

- Be appropriate for every client. The activities and client support strategies included in your plan are time consuming and require careful coordination. They cannot be effectively or efficiently applied to a large book of small clients that have little appreciation for the extra steps you will take and probably have little use for the added value that you will bring to the relationship. These plans are meant for larger, complex, long-term clients. They are not meant for low premium, price-focused, fickle clients.

Your value-added service plan will create a uniquely personalized foundation for mutually beneficial exchanges of value, integrity, and trust with those clients that are worthy of your time and attention. It will not prevent or predict human error or systems malfunctions, nor will it convert low-end clients into favorable ones. But it will give you an advantage over the rest of the field. I have noticed that when things do go wrong, practitioners of a value-added service philosophy, those that have created a more sophisticated level of client interaction and empathy, are able to easily insulate the client relationship from the service glitch.

They enjoy higher levels of client loyalty and lots of "wiggle-room" within the relationship because they have consistently demonstrated their commitment to their clients. They are forgiven for the small slips because they take care of the big stuff.

A final plug for consistency

Like Channel Marketing, providing value-added service requires consistency, patience, determination, and an honest desire to help. Because we have removed the sales event as the demilitarized zone between what is selling behavior and what is service behavior, the activities and tactics that we use to attract new clients and develop a relationship with them are the very same things that we will do to provide value-added service and continue to develop the relationship. On both sides of the initial transaction, our motive is the same and the desired result is identical—provide our clients with consistent and proactive demonstrations of value, integrity, and trust. The activities that we engage in to support this common objective should also be similar.

Can the system or plan serve a duel purpose? Absolutely. By design, the target marketing plan that you have created should also be equally effective as a value-added service plan. In fact, that is exactly what happens. Not only is the message and activity consistent from the first introduction to the last referral, you also save countless hours and huge redundancies by eliminating the need to manage separate sales and service functions.

When to start

The value-added service plan is essentially your client management strategy for your key accounts. Every qualified client receives a customized plan that is constructed to proactively fulfill each expectation that was identified during your needs assessment. Therefore, your plan is designed and presented to the client before any transaction takes place and usually before the client has selected you as a broker of record. Remember what you are selling—YOU and your ability to bring value, integrity, and trust to their insurance program. The client needs to see evidence of your ability prior to buying it.

The evidence is your value-added service plan. Your customized, proactive, client management plan that is designed specifically to reduce the frequency and severity of claims, prevent accidents and injuries, and reduce the cost of insurance over time—the right way. In helping to make the client company better, your plan will, in most cases, improve morale, reduce employee turnover, improve quality and service, and create new efficiencies.

These "softer" benefits result from the employees participating directly in the management of their insurance program and from taking a harder look at how and why they do what they do the way that they do it. They adopt a "critical eye" approach that breeds new ideas and creates new solutions to existing problems. It's empowering, dynamic, and extremely effective.

We know that the best way to manage insurance claims is to prevent them from ever happening. Our value-added service plan is used to schedule the action items we intend to deploy on a monthly basis to proactively manage the insurance program while continuing to build and maintain the client relationship. Here is how to create one:

Start by making a list of all activities that were identified during the needs assessment. In our Acme Cement example, these included:

1. Establish safety committee that meets monthly.
2. Establish and implement safe lifting standards.
3. Conduct twice-annual driver safety classes.
4. Conduct quarterly account reviews with team.
5. Attend safety committee meetings.
6. Conduct quarterly employee training.
7. Design customized workplace safety initiatives.
8. Establish emergency medical procedure.
9. Create standards for improving security and monitoring visitors.
10. Conduct scheduled reserve analysis with underwriters.

Next, add to the list any agency-wide initiatives that are planned and would be appropriate for the client. These might include:

1. Semi-annual Risk Management Workshops
2. Quarterly Client Roundtables
3. Monthly Electronic Client Newsletter
4. Annual Client Picnic
5. Semi-annual Needs Assessment Updates
6. Monthly Progress Reports

Finally, add any additional services that are specific to the client or conducted on an as-needed basis and do not need to be calendared. These might include:

1. Work with carrier and client to create needed risk management program templates.

2. Conduct specialized training for new safety committee.

3. Establish workplace safety incentive program.

4. Create and supply accident-reporting kits for vehicles.

5. Send weekly "check-in" emails to the safety program coordinators.

6. Post claims hot-line number in all departments.

7. Attend industry manufacturers' annual convention.

8. Maintain clipping file and forward as appropriate.

9. Request referrals.

10. Update and rehearse crisis management plan.

And so on. Your list of value-added services should be as comprehensive as possible without being overwhelming to either you or the client. These services and the schedule to deliver them are of little use to anybody if they cannot be effectively and efficiently facilitated. Nor should they be "fluffy". Your inherent value is your ability to manage a plan of activities that ultimately has a measurable, positive bottom-line impact on the client. Your visits have purpose and add value; they are not the drop-in-bring-donuts-to-say-I-was-there type of visit. Yes, we need to be visible; however it is equally necessary to remain viable.

To test the integrity of any particular event or activity, ask yourself "what purpose does it serve and what effect will it have?" If the purpose is definitive and the results are tangible and measurable, you have a winner. For instance, conducting bi-annual needs assessment updates will enable you to identify new exposures and expectations, make the necessary changes to your current plan, further enhance the organization's ability to proactively manage the insurance program, and help to eliminate the potential for service problems. It also gives you a chance to evaluate the client's perception of the service that you are providing and make any adjustments that are necessary. "Is what we are doing worth the time that we are spending?" is a question that can be asked and answered. The quarterly account reviews will allow everybody to take a step back from the program and evaluate progress against the program benchmarks. "Are we getting the results that we expected? Should we do more? Less? Different?" The answers to these questions will provide you with the information that you need to allocate and reallocate your most valuable asset—your time.

Take steps to emphasize the big picture. Make sure that they see your vision. When presenting this list of initiatives to the client, connect each one to an impact statement to ensure that they fully comprehend the value that you are providing. You, or a representative from your team, are not attending safety committee meetings just to be nice; you are doing so in order to train them and guide them to become a self-managed, proactive, viable, risk management team. Ultimately, they will reduce claims and the cost of the insurance program. And so it should be for each activity.

Having itemized the services and correlated each with a tangible result, the next step is to create an implementation schedule that you will present to the client. This is nothing more than pre-scheduling each activity into a monthly calendar, as follows:

Value Added Service Schedule for Acme Cement

January	February	March
Establish Safety Committee	Establish Safety Committee	Establish Safety Committee
Training – Slip Trip & Fall	Safe Lifting Program	Driver Safety Program
Client Roundtable	Agency Workshop	Account Review
Newsletter	Newsletter	Newsletter
Progress Report	Progress Report	Progress Report
Emergency Medical Plan Intro.	Visitor Security Intro.	Loss Control Visit
April	**May**	**June**
Safe Lifting Program	Attend Safety Committee	Account Review
Client Roundtable	Training – Sex Harassment	Newsletter
Newsletter	Newsletter	Client Picnic
Progress Report	Progress Report	Assessment Update
Reserve Analysis	Loss Control Visit	Progress Report
July	**August**	**September**
Attend Safety Committee	Driver Safety Program	Attend Safety Committee
Safe Lifting Program	Training - Diversity	Account Review
Client Roundtable	Agency Workshop	Newsletter
Newsletter	Newsletter	Progress Report
Progress Report	Progress Report	Loss Control Visit
October	**November**	**December**
Safe Lifting Program	Attend Safety Committee	Account Review
Client Roundtable	Training – Claims Reporting	Newsletter
Newsletter	Newsletter	Assessment Update
Progress Report	Progress Report	Progress Report
Reserve Analysis	Loss Control Visit	

Other Initiatives:

- Work with carrier and client to create needed risk management program templates.
- Conduct specialized training for new safety committee.
- Establish workplace safety incentive program.
- Create and supply accident-reporting kits for vehicles.
- Send weekly "check-in" emails to the safety program coordinators.
- Post claims hot-line number in all departments.
- Attend cement manufacturers annual convention.
- Maintain clipping file and forward as appropriate.
- Request referrals.
- Update and rehearse crisis management plan.

Now you have your plan—all scheduled and ready to deliver. Let's take a moment to acknowledge that this plan is a very involved and busy one—intended only for a client that is worthy of the time and attention, understands and appreciates the value that you will provide, and provides enough of a commission on the account to make it all worthwhile. Smaller, less complex accounts and personal lines accounts require a much more efficient, less intensive plan. The plan for a personal lines account may only involve monthly emails (done in a group for all clients), twice annual visits, a newsletter, quarterly phone account reviews, two client workshops, and a birthday card.

I recommend that you regularly evaluate the appropriate level of service for each account to ensure that you are getting compensated for your time. In short, there must be a "quid pro quo" established for every service plan. This does not mean that you charge fees. It does mean that you provide strategic levels of service only to those who are worthy of your time and attention: those who recognize your value and offer enough commission income to support the plan.

Also, be flexible. Consider the initial plan to be only a draft and, as you present it to the client, let it be known that you would like them to adjust it as they see fit. Is it too much? Too little? Rather than guess, ask. They will also want to add in some ideas of their own, which, upon delivery, will further enhance the perception of value.

Now, back to you.

How do you manage all of this activity efficiently and still sell? Let's start the discussion by remembering what you are selling—you are selling this plan and your commitment to it. The insurance product is important but it is only a piece of this much larger picture.

Let's assume that you have done the market research necessary to identify some key prospects for the coming year. You are also actively working your referral harvesting program. Through blending the two strategies, you have developed a prospect list of 25 key accounts that you intend to approach. Following the recommended steps outlined in the Channel Marketing and Referral Harvesting Sections, you send out your letters and include them on the list of invitees to your agency events (items 11-16 on your value-added service plan). Eventually, you gain an audience, administer the needs assessment, and create the prospect's value-added service plan. Regardless of the expiration date of the existing policy, the plan starts and you provide the services outlined. This may mean that a significant amount of time elapses before you actually take over the account at expiration date, or you could get a broker of record letter on day one. I actually prefer the delay because it leaves time to demonstrate the effectiveness of plan, build the value, and truly differentiate. If we have done our homework on the account and we trust that they fit our profile, then it is usually safe to invest our time and attention prior to getting paid. Most often, after seeing you in action, the account comes to you on a broker of record letter long before the hunting season arrives.

Managing The Value-Added Service Plans

Okay, you have created your plans for your key accounts (15 of them) and for your prospects (15 of them). You are faced with the daunting task of proactively managing 30 distinct plans and all that they contain. It appears to be overwhelming and, suddenly, you hate me. Understandable, if I stopped here, I'd hate me too. No need for that, as I'm going to give you the the greatest tool of the program—the one that we have been building to all along. The one that will allow you to incorporate everything that we have reviewed into a concise, coherent, consistent, and manageable format. It is a simple calendar of events, mapped out for the year, broken down into months, for easy integration into your weekly calendar and to-do list (Priority Management Section). In fact, the entire master value-added service plan for all 30 accounts (more if needed) can be contained on two pages. Here is an example, then we'll walk through how to build one for you.

Value-Added Service Plan

Client	JAN	FEB	MAR	APR	MAY	JUN
Acme	1,6,8,9	1,2,9,7	1,3,4,20	2,10,23	5,6,20,30	4,15,22,23
Client 2	5, 6, 16	15,18,21	4,10,20	5,16	6,18,28	4,17,20,32
Client 3	4,7,10	5,18,20	16,17,22	4,25,29	3,5,7,15	10,16,28
Client 4	6,18,28	4,16,23	5,10,25	3,7,21	4,6,16	18,25,30
Client 5	4,20,30	5,6,21	7,16,28	4,15	5,10	6,18
Client 6	5,7	4,10	6,15	5,20	4,7,30	6,28,31
Client 7	6,15	7,8,18	4,16	5,29	6,20	4,10,31
Client 8	4,6	5,15	7,20	4,10,18	5,16	7,28
Client 9	5,10	4,6	7,15	5,16,30	4,18	6,17
Client 10	7,28	8,18	4,5	6,31	9,15	4
Client 11	4	7,16	6,10	4,18	5,20	6,30
Client 12	6	4,28	5,17,30	10,29	4,18	5,20
Client 13	9,18	10,30	4	5,15	6,31	4,28
Client 14	16	5,21	6	4	7,30	10
Client 15	4	20	18	6	4	16
Prospect 1	33	15,10,18	4,7,20	1,6,20	1,21,25,18	4,26,23
Prospect 2	33	33	33	33	15,10,18	7
Prospect 3	33,26	33	15,10,18	4,7,20		
Prospect 4	33	33	33	17	33	33
Prospect 5	33	15,10,18	4,7,20			26
Prospect 6	33	33	33	33	15,10,18	4,7,20
Prospect 7	15,10,18	4,7,20				
Prospect 8	33	33	33	15,10,18	4,7,20	
Prospect 9	33	33	33	33	33	33,17
Prospect 10	33	15,10,18	4,7,20		26	
Prospect 11	33	33	33	33	33	33,26
Prospect 12	33	33	33	33	33	33
Prospect 13	15,10,18	4,7,20				
Prospect 14	33	33	33	15,10,18	4,7,20	
Prospect 15	33	33	33	33	33	15,10,18

Value-Added Service Plan

Client	JUL	AUG	SEP	OCT	NOV	DEC
Acme	2,5,25,26		5,4,20	2,10,29	5,6,20	4,15,31
Client 2	5,16		4,6,26	5,16,29	10,18,20	4,6,31
Client 3	4,18,21		5,16	4,21,15	3,18,31	5,16,20
Client 4	5,10,21		3,16	18,32	4,6,31	7,22,15
Client 5	4,16		7,15	4,18	6,21	5,10,16
Client 6	5,10		6	5,15	4	21,30
Client 7	7,15		4,18	6,28	21,30	4
Client 8	4,6,31		5,30	4,10,18	7,16	5,21
Client 9	5,21		15,16	6,28	4,18	20
Client 10	7,20		4,18	6,30	15	4
Client 11	4,16		5,21	4,31	6	18
Client 12	6,31		15	5,21	4	16
Client 13	7,30		4,18	6,20	15	4
Client 14	4,17		20	4,18	28	15
Client 15	5,21		4,31	28	7	10,15
Prospect 1	5,7,15		4,22	5,18	28	4,6
Prospect 2	17			15		
Prospect 3						
Prospect 4	15,10		1			
Prospect 5						
Prospect 6			15			
Prospect 7						
Prospect 8						
Prospect 9	33		7			
Prospect 10					15	
Prospect 11	33		15,10,18	4,7,20		
Prospect 12	33		33	15,10	4,7,20	
Prospect 13	15					
Prospect 14					15	
Prospect 15	4,7,20					15

Value-Added Service Activities

1. Establish safety committee that meets monthly.
2. Establish and implement safe lifting standards.
3. Conduct driver safety classes.
4. Conduct account reviews with team.
5. Attend safety committee meetings.
6. Conduct employee training.
7. Design customized workplace safety initiatives.
8. Establish emergency medical procedure.
9. Create standards for improving security and monitoring visitors.
10. Conduct scheduled reserve analysis with underwriters.
11. Conduct Semi-annual Risk Management Workshops.
12. Conduct Quarterly Client Roundtables.
13. Send Monthly Electronic Client Newsletter.
14. Attend Annual Client Picnic.
15. Send Needs assessment updates.
16. Claims Reviews.
17. Participate in client charity drive.
18. Conduct on-site visit with underwriter.
19. Send Monthly Progress Reports
20. Work with carriers and clients to create needed risk management program templates.
21. Conduct specialized training safety committees.
22. Establish workplace safety incentive programs.
23. Create and supply accident-reporting kits for vehicles.
24. Send weekly "check-in" emails to the safety program coordinators.
25. Post claims hot-line number in all client offices.
26. Attend Client Association Meetings and Industry annual convention.
27. Maintain clipping file and forward as appropriate.
28. Request referrals.
29. Update and rehearse crisis management plans.
30. Send Birthday Cards and Holiday Cards to all Clients.
31. Conduct a Detailed Client Survey once/Year with all Clients.
32. Send Service Letter, Make Service Call, or Send Greeting Card for non-contact months.
33. Send pre-approach letter and other correspondence.

Weekly Activities for all:	24 (Emails to safety coordinators)
Monthly Activities for all:	13 (Newsletter), 19 (Progress Report)
Quarterly Activities for all:	12 (Roundtables)
Semi-Annual Activities for all:	11 (Risk Management Workshop)
Annual Activities for all:	14 (Client Picnic - July),
	32 (Holiday Card - December)
Unscheduled Activities for all:	32 (Service letter, service call, card)
	33 (Send pre-approach letter and other correspondence)

This example of a "master" value-added service plan is a roll-up of every individual value-added service schedule that was custom developed for each client and potential client. It is a snapshot of all scheduled client management activities for the year and, used effectively, it is the "coup-de-grace" of differentiation. The plan will allow you to proactively coordinate all activities with all service providers and carriers, track performance against established benchmarks, and correlate your activity to a bottom-line impact within the client company.

The plan shown above is an elaborate one that is loaded with activities that require an audience with the client or prospect. While your plan may not be as involved, the impact and the client's perception of value will be similar when presented. This positive effect specifically results from the proactive, well planned, customized approach that you are taking. Notice that none of the activities are "spectacular" or especially unique—many can be considered normal account management events that you have seen before and may currently practice. In and of themselves, they do not effectively differentiate you from other service-focused producers. Instead, it is the strategically laid-out plan, the proactive and predictable approach that ties it all together and creates the added value.

Take care not to over-allocate your resources. Your most limited resource, your time, must be carefully preserved and only invested in activities with clients that are worthy of the attention. You cannot be everything to everybody nor should you try to be. This level of account management is not appropriate for clients that don't value it (regardless of the size of the account) or for those that can't "pay" for it because their premium levels are too low.

Be very, very careful to adequately segment your book of business and plan accordingly. The opportunity cost associated with not doing so is horrific. If you are investing time in over-servicing an account, you are taking time away from another account where your impact and value could be much greater. So pick your spots and pick them carefully.

Notice that on the sample plan, the clients and prospects are "ranked", 1–15. Notice too that the level of contact and service is most intense and complex at the top of the plan and becomes less involved as you work the plan down to number 15. This is not accidental—it is strategic. Generally, the larger the account, the greater the impact, and the more time and attention that is warranted.

Constructing your plan starts with an unbiased segmentation of your existing book of business and your list of prospects. We are going to rank each account based upon two criteria:

1. Size of account and potential for opportunity.
2. Perception of value for services and cultural compatibility.

Size of account and potential for opportunity

We get paid for what we are worth—once we prove our worth. Our plan recognizes this and understands that nobody works this hard for free so you must be compensated for your time. Obviously commissions are higher for larger accounts and these clients should merit a higher ranking providing that they meet the cultural compatibility requirement and appreciate the value that you are bringing to the table. Opportunity, however comes in many guises. For instance, suppose that you have approached a sizable client and they, being impressed by your message, have given you a piece of the overall account—perhaps just one line of business. They might be testing you, they might have scattered expiration dates for different lines, or maybe they have to "ease" their way out of an existing relationship with an incumbent broker or carrier. On paper, the account isn't too impressive; however, the potential to round it out as the relationship progresses could be magnificent and therefore would merit a higher degree of time and attention that might otherwise have been allocated.

Centers-of-influence should also experience your premier service plan for it is they who will endorse you, encourage you, educate you, and lead you to your cornerstone accounts. They need to know how good you are and you need to show them how good you can be.

Some suggest that you could and should charge fees beyond the commission for these value-driven account management activities. Some discount the commission at time of sale and charge a "pay-as-you-go" account management fee. The fact that this is a common technique indicates that there are circumstances where it can be applied successfully. Personally, I believe that this practice greatly diminishes the perception of value that is the foundation of your message and it too often focuses the client on what they are paying rather than what you are doing. It's your call.

Perception of value for services and cultural compatibility

Sometimes, large companies don't translate into large commissions. Likewise, a large account does not automatically qualify as a "good" account. A "good" account is one that is able to rise above the narrow confines of the common "insurance is about price and product" perspective and view the entire insurance program. Good accounts will comprehend the inherent value of your plan and its positive implications for their organization. At some level, they view you as a "partner" rather than a policy pusher and they will actively participate in the development and implementation of the insurance program. Price will matter, but it will be considered as a part of the overall landscape rather than a world unto itself, only one of many factors that will enter into the buying decision rather than the single greatest one. Good accounts want you to actively and consistently participate in managing your program, while other accounts would prefer to be left alone unless something breaks.

Agreement to and participation in the needs assessment provides you with a clear indication as to which side of the line the account is likely to fall, but it is no guarantee. Most people and companies are somewhere in between the extremes of what constitutes a "good" and "bad" account and most can be moved up the scale and get better over time—providing that they are willing and able.

With these two qualifiers in mind, segment your book of business and rank your clients. I use a simple system to grade each client, as follows:

A – Great Opportunity, Culturally Compatible

B – Good Opportunity, Culturally Compatible

C – Great Opportunity, Culturally Questionable

D – Small Opportunity, Culturally Compatible

E – Good Opportunity, Culturally Questionable

Your ranking system is customizable and completely up to you. The objective is to scale your book of business so that you can efficiently allocate your resources. If you are concerned that you have not done a needs assessment on some or all of your existing clients and cannot make a fair or convincing assessment of their potential or compatibility—now is a good time to set the appointment and get the process going. Even if you have a good feel for your clients and how to rank them, conduct the needs assessment on those that have not had it yet as a first step to introducing your account management strategy. You'll be shocked to discover how many once dormant accounts suddenly spring to life around your program.

Having segmented the book, it is time to take a hard look at the accounts on the low tiers. We have previously acknowledged that we cannot be all things to all people, that investing our time and attention with those clients who are most worthy necessarily means less or no time spent with those that are not. Now we are looking at the lowest tier of our segmentation plan, made up of our worst performing and least compatible accounts, and it's not a pretty sight, especially since some of these accounts are also our noisiest. Administratively unorganized and risk management inept, their service "program" has historically been limited to responding to the crisis of the moment, in the moment. These are the clients that put the "fun" in dysfunction—always needy, always late, always reactive, always calling, sometimes rude, perpetually non-renewed, rarely loyal, and never learning. In short, they're a pain in the ass. The commission that we make hardly covers the cost of the time that they take.

What to do, what to do …

End it. Retaining these accounts is asking for trouble in a hard market where profitability means leverage and favorable treatment with every carrier. Move them to a service center or TPA, suggest another broker, give them to a new producer to cut their teeth on, or provide them with administrative services only and cut off any access to your time. At this end of your book, you simply cannot afford to give too much and have your best accounts suffer as a result.

Building a book of business should not mean building an ever-expanding client list—keeping all that you have and constantly pushing to add more. This common business practice is what causes most of the traditional problems with effective account management to begin with. Rather than focusing on our number of clients, our strategy demands that we continue to focus on quality and size of clients. By keeping our number of clients consistent by replacing poor performing or poorly qualified accounts with larger and better, we can steadily grow our book without cheating anybody, including ourselves.

Practicing this strategy might someday make today's middle-of-the-pack account your worst performer. That's fine. In fact, what does that tell you about the quality and the performance of the accounts that you have built on top of this one? It should tell you that you have done a masterful job of focusing on the right relationships while building new ones. It is a privilege to work with you, to have access to your time and limited resources. It is a privilege and not an entitlement. Manage yourself and your book of business accordingly.

Once you have decided which of your key accounts and key prospects are going to receive your value-added program, list them in ranked order on the right side of your activity management calendar as shown in the example. Now it is time to fill in the activities.

Planning the service activity

At this point you have lists of activities created from nearly every chapter in the book. You have also created client specific activities after conducting each needs assessment. Collectively, it's a lot of stuff, stuff that needs to be organized efficiently.

Start by making a master list of all of the activities that you have created. Assign each activity a number as shown in the sample, which contains thirty-three value-added service activities. Some of these activities will be applied universally across the client list. Others have limited or specialized application, resulting from a specific need that arose from an assessment. Some can be generalized rather than appearing specifically as described in the client's individual plan. In our example, *Acme Cement* has specific training topics listed on the individual plan; however, the activity shows up as "Conduct Employee Training" (Item 6) on the master list. However you design your master list, make it functional, keep it to one page.

You now know what you are going to do and you have identified to whom you are going to do it. Let's determine when you will do it by calendering the activities and events. Here are the steps:

Identify the scheduled activities that are unilateral and consistent. The activities that apply to everyone at consistent intervals throughout the year (in our example, these are activities numbers **11, 12, 13, 14, 19, 24, 32**). Although these activities definitely appear on the individual client plans, we are footnoting them on the master plan to avoid unnecessary clutter on the matrix.

Identify unscheduled activities that will be deployed on an as-needed or random basis (in our example this is activity **33**). Once again, to avoid unnecessary clutter, we have elected to footnote these activities on the master plan.

Next, use the individual value-added service schedules that you created for each client and place the activity codes in the appropriate month of delivery for each existing client. Notice in our example that the higher ranking clients receive more face-time and more services than the others do. As you work your way down the list, the activity becomes less frequent and less complex.

Finally, after ranking your prospects using the same criteria that we used when evaluating our existing clients, we plot out their contact schedule and marketing touches which lead up to an estimated time for their initial needs assessment. After conducting the needs assessment, we will be in an informed enough position to build out the remainder of their plan (as shown with "Prospect 1") on our sample plan. We can also safely predict the activity for any new account in the first few months following the needs assessment and these events are also shown; however, that is all we can safely anticipate at this point. Keep in mind that the "blank" months are not truly empty—we will continue to provide all of the footnoted activity each month, as appropriate.

When allocating your time and attention and determining the level of services that are appropriate for each client, be conservative. Though the needs assessment may have uncovered a long list of issues in need of attention and some significant holes in the current program, you cannot fix it all at once. Pace yourself, pace your client, prioritize the objectives, and stretch out the initiatives to ensure that you can manage the program consistently and effectively. Some objectives will have to wait and they may have to wait until years two, three, and four of the program.

This is not to suggest that we abandon the lower ranking clients or those that do not make the master value-added service plan. The weekly, monthly, quarterly, semi-annual and annual activities are intended for every client and meet our objective for consistent client contact over time. Additionally, these unilateral activities add a significant level of value on their own and are the core activities for prospects contained in our marketing plan. If these baseline activities successfully attracted clients, they will also retain them. Let's be clear on this—no client is getting cheated. All are getting the level of service that is appropriate for their circumstances.

You now have your plan and you are equipped with the tools that you will need to execute the plan consistently. Similar to your weekly plans that were created in the chapter on priority management, your master plan and the individual plans are going to remain fluid rather than fixed. We have created our plans based only on what we know to be true for today and on what we can reasonably expect to occur in the future. We are never exact with our forecast nor should we be too confident in our assumptions and expectations. You will change, clients will change, underwriters will change, the market will change … and so on. Everything will adjust and you will need to make adjustments. Not all of your highest ranking clients will respond as expected and, as such they will need to move down in ranking. Conversely, some clients that currently rank lower will absorb you, respond to you, and perform for you. These you will move higher.

You'll not be successful with every prospect and your pool of prospects will change as time rolls on. New ideas will creep into your plan, new value-drivers that will develop from your experience and from that of your clients. Some established activities will fade due to ineffectiveness and/or inefficiency. In short, you'll grow, your clients will grow, their needs will change, and your plan will change to accommodate. That is how it should be.

Not shown in our plan are the inevitable ad-hoc meetings that you will have to have with clients, underwriters, prospects, and colleagues. Not shown in our plan are the day-to-day administrative tasks that are inevitable. Not shown in our plan are the crises, the phone calls and other interruptions that require you to drop what you are doing and spring into action. Not shown is a perfect plan.

What is shown is an account management process that, though flexible, will keep you focused on doing the right things, in the right way, for the right reason, with the right people. What is shown is a way out of the traditional sales and service model that defeats too many and benefits too few. What is shown is a proven formula for achieving a level of success beyond your wildest dreams, in a hard market like this one or in a soft market that will someday follow this one. What is shown, in combination with all that I have shown you throughout this book, is the best possible advice I will ever give—and, quite possibly, the best and most rewarding advice you'll ever receive.

Now we move on to our final chapter. You have established your objectives and created a priority management system that will direct your personal and professional activities toward their achievement. You have researched and analyzed the marketplace and designed a service-driven channel marketing system that will attract and embrace the clients that are worthy of your time and attention. You have created a comprehensive needs assessment for these clients that enables you to reach far beyond the issues of policy and price to custom-develop a proactive, tangible risk management program for each of them. Using this information, you have produced a value-added service plan that establishes performance benchmarks, specifically defines activities and schedules contacts, and correctly manages insurance program cost by proactively managing the frequency and severity of claims.

You have done it all and done it well. Your client and carrier relationships have evolved to become partnerships and you are now in a position to reap the rewards of doing the right thing, in the right way, for the right reasons, with the right people. It is time to harvest.

Chapter Nine:

Referral Harvesting:
The Grand Finale

*"The way to gain a good reputation is to endeavor
to be what you desire to appear."*
— Socrates

There's an old Chinese proverb that says it takes two wings for a bird to fly. Loosely translated, that means you'll travel much farther in life if you build relationships with people who you can help—and who can help you.

In our line of work that means getting referrals. And to get referrals, you must build a reputation as a sincere and consistent creator and provider of insurance programs that truly make a difference for your clients. A difference that is measurable, visible, and viable. The trick is not only to build that relationship, but to do so in a manner where your clients understand your value, respect your integrity, and trust your ability. Once this is done, you will discover that they will have an inherent desire to do more for you—to go beyond the commission to reward you for your professional friendship and loyalty to their cause. Affording them the opportunity to provide you with a referral satisfies this desire and is the greatest business-building method that you have at your disposal.

In fact, referral harvesting is also the most efficient and cost effective prospecting strategy that you can engage in. Referrals from clients, centers-of-influence, and industry friends are the most expedient route to meeting prospects who have an established need and are looking for a trustworthy solution.

How? For starters, think of your professional network as a "referral garden". It's a clear way to visualize that you have to plant the seeds (build relationships), pull the weeds (eliminate the time wasters), nurture your business contacts (grow the relationships), and harvest them when the time is right (ask for referrals), just as you would working in your backyard garden. Your referral garden is actually your most valuable business asset. It is your most reliable source for new business development and it is your only source for renewal and cross-selling premium. As is true of any garden, however, you can only reap what you sow.

What's the key to a thriving referral garden? At the top of the list is the caliber of your relationships with existing clients, centers, and professional friends. That, more than most factors, will determine the quality and quantity of the available referrals. If you have nurtured your contacts and clients well by consistently and proactively delivering value, integrity, and trust; you will have an unlimited supply of qualified referrals to harvest. If you haven't, you won't.

Long before I was able to capitalize on this simple tenet, in those "hamster in a wheel" days of running hard and working stupid, I did recognize that the few referrals that did come my way were much more accommodating than the introductions that I was creating on my own (even a broken clock is right twice a day). In most cases, the referred prospects were willing to at least let me quote their account and in all cases I was granted an audience. Occasionally, I even sold something. Compared against the dismal results generated by my traditional marketing programs, referral harvesting was, even then, the most tolerable of all selling methods. Imagining a selling system where the business came to me, pre-qualified and prepared to start the courtship, I knew right then I was onto something—something big.

I was right. In the years that have passed between those days and this one, I have come to rely on referrals as the sole source of supply for new business opportunities. I have done so by steadfastly investing my time and attention in the client companies that have embraced me as a partner and call me their friend. That said, the new clients that have come to me from the referrals would not have materialized, at least not consistently so, if I hadn't first planned a deliberate system for harvesting the referrals that were readily available. Meaning, I had to ask for them.

The "asking" thing is the part of the process that proves the most challenging for all but a few producers that I have met. When I am speaking at producer gatherings and industry conventions, I will often ask members of the audience to raise their hand if they consistently ask for two to three referrals each week. Invariably, the results of this informal poll are 5% or less. Not surprisingly, the same results are found at the agency level.

This behavior flies in the face of all that is logical. Frankly, what we are really saying is that we would prefer to dance on the head of a pin in order to win the business of a perfect stranger rather than receive a warm introduction to a better qualified opportunity. Why?

Mark Twain once said, "Man is the only animal that blushes. Or needs to." Meaning of course, that we are naturally self-conscious, fear embarrassment and rejection, and are capable at any moment of committing a social blunder that will validate the reasoning for the fear. It is this vicious psycho-social circle that has a lot to do with our reluctance to ask for referrals. Even when we know that our relationships are healthy and sound, even when we are sure that we have made a significant contribution, even when we have invested countless hours and significant money in marketing programs designed to attract the same potential clients that we could be introduced to directly, we are still uncomfortable asking for a referral.

Even today, after over a decade of using a "referral only" new business building strategy, I still bristle when the time has arrived to pop the question. I believe it is a natural reaction to the fear of being rejected by someone that I trust and value. If I listen to the fear and give into it, I can justify my lack of referral activity, invariably using one or more of the following excuses:

"I do not want to appear needy or pushy."

"I always forget to ask."

"They will not send me to their competitors."

"It feels unprofessional."

"It violates the nature of our relationship."

"I get them without asking."

"It's not the right time."

"They don't know anybody."

"I'm too busy as it is."

As George Costanza said once in *Seinfeld*, "yadda, yadda, yadda". I know the real reason—I am mortified at the thought of being rejected. I also fear that I have not done *everything* that I could do for the client and worry that I might not be entitled to a recommendation. Ultimately I had to learn that these anxieties are born out of a misunderstanding of the true nature of a referral, insufficient experience with a professional referral harvesting system, and a lack of exposure to the psychological benefits a client receives when he or she is asked for a referral. Once I was able to see the referral harvesting process for what it really is—a valid service technique as well as a prospecting strategy—I instantly became more comfortable with the idea and learned to counteract the anxiety with a rational approach.

The remainder of this chapter will help you to effectively eliminate these unnecessary encumbrances and provide you with a foundation to build your own personalized referral harvesting program.

Referral Magic

Why will new clients do business with you instead of somebody else? As we reviewed in the Channel Marketing chapter, their decision is based on your ability to communicate and demonstrate a level of value, integrity, and trust that overshadows your competition. Allow me to provide an example. You may not know the name Cyrus McCormick, but he helped invent the reaper. It wasn't the first such tool ever patented, but McCormick made sure to offer customers an installment plan and a money-back guarantee, which made a big name for himself and swept away his competition. Pretty soon, word got around that if you were in the market for a reaper, Cyrus was the man to see. Old Cyrus's marketing system was designed specifically—just like yours is—for this purpose by providing his prospects with gradual exposure to his message and consistent evidence of his sincerity. The major drawback to any marketing effort, including our own, is the time required to establish the credibility necessary to convince the prospect that you are for real.

Enter the referral. Here, the key is being viewed by prospective clients as a "known commodity" like Cyrus McCormick. Known commodities jump right to the front of the line when clients began making decisions on who gets their business. The fact that you are being recommended verifies to the new contact that you are reliable and proven; allowing you to avoid most, if not all, of the credibility-building steps in the relationship development process. Being a known commodity helps in other timesaving ways as well. Referral contacts are typically decision-makers so you do not waste valuable time working your way through layers of bureaucracy. This elevator goes straight to the top. As a known commodity you are talking with people whose interest you have attracted. They want to hear what you have to say and see what you can do. You are projected directly into the heart of the needs development stage of the relationship. No marketing chicken dance, no serenading, no bidding, and no nonsense.

Why are these recommendations held in such high regard by your prospects? Unlike all of the untried and untested claims of your competitors, somebody that they know has tested you. If the prospect values the opinion of the referral provider and trusts that their judgement is sound, the prospect will extend that trust and value to you as well.

Referrals that Service

How do you feel after you see an inspiring movie, dine at a sensational restaurant, or read an extraordinary book? Are you quiet about your experience or do you like to talk about it? How do you react when you are asked for a recommendation regarding the movie, restaurant, or book? Are you non-committal or do you enthusiastically give your opinion? Most of us are excited to share our positive experiences and we actively encourage others to accept our endorsements. We do this to be helpful and we do this as a way to validate our opinion. Without any particular allegiance to the producer of the movie, the chef at the restaurant, or the author of the book, I will make a recommendation and actively seek any feedback. If the feedback is positive, I will feel even better about my initial experience. This phenomenon plays a large role in counteracting buyer's remorse and it is why most of your clients will give you a referral if you ask them.

The fact is, we all have a need to share our opinions and positive experiences with others. This is true of your clients and their experiences with you as well. When we asked 3,000 commercial insurance purchasers what their response would be if approached for a referral, here is what they told us:

> 86% would give a referral if asked.
> 40% would give more than one referral.
> *Only 4%* had ever been asked for a referral.

Of the 14% that would not give a referral ...

> 85% indicated that they could not think of anybody at the time.
> 10% said that they did not give referrals.
> 5% said that the service could not be recommended.

So ... why the hesitation? Your clients are waiting for you to ask them and they are eager to help. Sounds like a no-brainer, right? But obviously it isn't—and that calls for a closer look. Knowing what we know now, let's review the most common justifications that we use for not asking for referrals and respond to each one.

"I do not want to appear needy or pushy." – Okay, fine. The reality is that your clients are the ones that are needy. They need you to ask them and they would push you to do so if you provide them with the opportunity. They need to know that their opinion matters to you and to others and they need to reinforce their decision to do business with you. You will actually improve your relationship by asking for their recommendation by allowing them to give back and help you, too.

"I always forget to ask." – Sorry, but this is a cop out. The remainder of this section will detail a referral harvesting system that is easy to use and easy to remember.

"They will not send me to their competitors." – This one I hear a lot. The fact is, you don't know who they know and you don't know where they will send you. Actually, I've been referred to a client's friendly competitor on numerous occasions and I also know that my clients share referral information with each other on a regular basis. In fact, it is what they talk about the most.

"It feels unprofessional." – That depends on how you ask, when you ask, and what you do after you ask. Referral requests can be handled unprofessionally—usually by those that don't belong in our profession. The difference will become clear as we describe our system.

"It violates the nature of our relationship." – Yes it does, for the better. Nobody has ever lost a client as a result of asking for a referral.

"I get them without asking." – Excellent. This is a good indicator of sound and healthy client relationships. How many more would you get if you asked for them rather than waiting for them?

"It's not the right time." – This answer only works if you have no clients and no network. Otherwise, it is always the right time. And remember also that procrastination is the thief of time.

"They don't know anybody." – You'll be amazed at who they know. They can also tell you who not to work with. Do not prejudge the answer to your referral request.

"I'm too busy as it is." – Too busy doing what? Referral harvesting is the fast and efficient track to new business development.

How NOT to Request a Referral

One of my first facilitations of our sales training program was with a group of whole-life producers from a giant mutual insurance company.

When I inquired about their volume of referral requests, the response was that they were required to ask for a minimum of three referrals at every appointment with every prospect and client. They had been trained not to leave the appointment until they had secured the referrals and they had developed an elaborate script that was intentionally designed to pressure the client or prospect into coughing up the names. Additionally, they each sent out quarterly mailings, disguised as customer service surveys, containing yet further referral solicitations.

Not surprisingly, this producer group was required to make 100 cold calls per day, push to close all prospects on the first meeting, and only schedule appointments to get a check and an application. Service calls were out of the question, relationships were non-existent, and anybody with a checkbook that was not at death's door was considered a potential client.

I had landed in producer hell. The entire sales process had to be re-tooled and the existing sales culture completely abandoned. One of our primary objectives was to transform the referral bludgeoning process into a referral harvesting system.

As we have already reviewed, clients provide qualified referrals for two primary reasons:

1. They feel that they have received something extraordinary, something special, and they wish to reinforce this belief by sharing it with others and receiving validation.

2. The producer has demonstrated a unique level of value, integrity, and trust that is often considered to be above and beyond the call of duty. The relationship is personal—a professional friendship—and the client wishes to help the producer become more successful.

In the case of this insurance company, neither condition was present. When I asked them what their impressions were of the referral program, they labeled it unprofessional and intrusive—rightfully so. They also found it to be terribly unproductive due to a high frequency of unqualified referrals. One of them had even been referred to a prospect's paperboy, another to an estranged ex-wife, and more than a few mentioned referrals to the deceased. Talk about dead ends.

There is a right way and a wrong way to do it and clearly this is the wrong way. However, let's not throw the baby out with the bath water.

Who to ask, when to ask, and how to ask

The cornerstone of any referral program is the strength of the relationship that you have forged with the referral provider. No relationship, no referral. Therefore, we do not ask for a referral until we have successfully, sincerely, and consistently demonstrated a value-added commitment to the referral provider and he or she has acknowledged our effort.

An effective referral harvesting system is set up and managed in the same way as the other prospecting systems that we have reviewed. Start by making a list of all existing clients, centers-of-influence, and other market service providers that you have developed a relationship with. This is your target market within a target market.

Next, set a weekly referral request objective. Of course your objective will depend on the number of names on your list, but, a minimum of one request per week is your goal. Don't worry about a lack of referral candidates—you haven't made it this far in sales without accumulating a stack of business cards from networking contacts. If you do not have at least twenty potential referral sources listed, it can only mean that you are new to the industry and the agency. Your list can begin with internal referral sources—friends and colleagues that are willing to introduce you to centers-of-influence, industry contacts, and potential clients.

With referrals, your timing counts. The most obvious time to make the request is during a service review conference with the client or during a pre-renewal meeting. These events are usually retrospective in nature and present a wonderful opportunity to acknowledge the value and good will that you have brought to the relationship. Additionally, you are face-to-face with the referral provider which adds credibility and professionalism to your request, enables you to better qualify or define whom you would like to meet, and allows you to help your client think through the introduction. Finally, your clients will often feel compelled to pick up the phone and make the introduction for you then and there. Like I said, people want to help you.

Don't ignore any opportunity to earn a referral. Often, referral request opportunities occur during normal conversations with your client or with a center-of-influence. Whether or not you are talking on the telephone or face-to-face, anytime the topic of discussion is about the service that you provide, the value that you have established, or the positive impact that you've made, circumstances are right for you to find out who else might benefit from your capability.

Be direct about it. I'll schedule a client meeting where the primary agenda is requesting a referral. I'll call the client or center-of-influence, request some time over breakfast or lunch, and clearly state that the reason for our meeting is to discuss new opportunities that they can recommend. Prior to the meeting, I send a list of prospective new accounts along with a profile of my typical client. This premeditated approach alerts the client to my intention, allows each of us to prepare, and sets the stage for a positive outcome.

As I've already mentioned, the act of "popping the question" is what many producers find most vexing. Tedious as it may seem, scripting the question and preparing to field the response is a great way to relieve some of this self-imposed pressure. Additionally, scripting the request will help you to qualify the referral and remind the referral provider that they will be recommending the value, integrity, and trust that is the foundation of your relationship. They will not be recommending an insurance product.

A typical request contains five or six key components that vary according to your circumstances and personal style. When preparing to script your referral request, you must plan to either ask in person or over the phone. If you are meeting or calling specifically to ask for a referral, your script begins by disclosing your intention (step 1). If your request will fit into another meeting or conversation, your script begins with the relationship reminder (step 2). The remaining steps can be inserted in any order that feels comfortable to you, with the exception of step 6. Regardless of the circumstances, never solicit referrals through the mail. Mailed requests are impersonal and unprofessional.

Your script should contain the following elements:

Step 1 – A disclosure of your intention:

Indicate clearly that you are calling or wish to meet about referrals.

Step 2 – A relationship reminder:

Reinforce the importance of the existing relationship.

Step 3 – A professional request:

Don't beat around the bush or hint at the question.

Step 4 – A qualifying statement:

"Who do you know like yourself?" or "Who could you recommend in the industry?"

Step 5 – Reassurance and assistance:

Take the pressure off and help them think.

Step 6 – A professional thank you and a commitment to follow-up.

Here is an example of a telephone request:
(Producer)
"Hi Bob, this is Scott Primiano, do you have a moment?"
(Client)
"Yes"
(Producer)
"The reason I called, Bob, is to ask for your help. I truly respect your opinion and I would like you to recommend another organization like your own, who would benefit from the same level of service that I have provided to you over the past few years. My intent, Bob, is to continue to develop my business, but I would not do so at the expense of our relationship, so if you don't feel comfortable, this is not critical."

Before we proceed any further, let's spend some time reviewing Bob's potential responses to my request. As we indicated earlier, 80% of the time we will be given a referral. If this were to occur with Bob, I would immediately move into a "thank you and follow-up" strategy that will appropriately acknowledge the goodwill that Bob has extended to me. However, what if the answer is not the one that we were hoping for? In fact, what if Bob's response is the answer that we feared the most—a flat out rejection?

Do we?:

A) Run away and stay away.

B) Never ask for a referral again.

C) Pretend that we were joking.

D) All of the above.

E) None of the above.

The correct answer is, of course, "none of the above". The truth is that *any* answer to a referral request can be a positive one providing that we respond appropriately by doing something constructive with the information that we have been given. For example, Bob says:
"Scott, I can't think of anybody", or, "I really don't know anybody."

My first reaction is likely to be "Uh-Oh". My instincts will tell me that something bad has happened. I will interpret Bob's message to be a polite "no" and I will feel the urge to mumble a "good-bye" and hang up, or change the topic and pretend it never happened (Say Bob, how'bout dem Red Sox?"). In the time it takes for your body to process its "fight or flight" response—a second or so—I will be flooded with negative impressions of Bob's response that will be, at best, uncomfortable. Worse yet, if the moment is allowed to awkwardly hang where it is, Bob will sense my reaction and immediately become uncomfortable as well. So … I need to act.

First, I must realize that Bob's answer is perfectly legitimate. I called him out of the blue and asked him a very important, thought provoking question. I also know that Bob was hardly hanging by the phone, wringing his hands in despair because I hadn't called and asked him for a referral yet. So what on earth would lead me to expect that he would be able to offer a quality recommendation on the spot?

Second, I have to ignore my initial reaction. My feelings of rejection and disappointment are conditioned responses to an unrealized expectation. However natural they may be, they are inappropriate for this situation and of absolutely no help to me.

Third, I need to help Bob think. He wants to help me, he's feeling awkward about not being able to help me, and he needs me to help him help me. Therefore, my response to Bob must be supportive rather than evasive. I'm obligated to clarify my question by providing Bob with enough information to make an educated decision about where to refer me. This may take time and involve tactful follow-up.

For example, my response to

"Scott, I would love to help, however I can't think of anyone"
may be:

"That's understandable, I called out of the blue. Many of my clients refer me to indirect competitors, industry associates, vendors, and their clients. Why don't I give you some time to think about it and follow up with you next week?"

OR

"Many of my clients refer me to indirect competitors, industry associates, vendors, and their clients. I have a list of organizations that meet my client profile and that I would like to be introduced to. Perhaps we can we review it together and see who you might recognize or I can e-mail it to you and we can talk over the phone?"

My replies are specifically designed to take the temperature gauge down a notch and remove any pressure that Bob might be feeling and to move beyond an immediate "yes" or "no" answer.

It's a good idea to brace yourself and be prepared for some immediate variation of the word "no". For example, a client will occasionally answer my request for a referral with "I don't give referrals". My reaction to this type of answer is apt to be even more negative and defensive than the previous scenario, and I will definitely feel like it's a brush off. As before, however, I must override my instinctive urge to run away and consider more carefully why my client has closed the door on referral requests. Chances are very good that the client, Bob in this case, has had a bad experience with a referral before and is reluctant to stick his neck out again. Perhaps Bob is friendly with other agents and prefers not to give special treatment to any one of us. Maybe he is just not comfortable with the idea and really would prefer to keep me a secret. Whatever the reason, I need to find out.

With this in mind, my follow-up to this response is a simple question:

"Oh, I wasn't aware of that. Why don't you give referrals?"

Inevitably, I will learn about the reasons for his resistance and, instead of combating them, I will support them. The idea here is to remove any hint of tension. I do not want to be in a position that requires me to justify why I'm worthy of his recommendation nor do I ever want to "sell" him into giving me a referral. Regardless of his rational, this is Bob's decision and I must respect his position rather than argue against it. My reply to his explanation will be an empathetic one such as:

"Oh, that makes sense, I understand completely."

Once again, I have taken the pressure off of the situation and allowed Bob to stay within his comfort zone. However, my work is not done.

Bob is going to have some guilt. At some level, he'll feel inadequate because he will believe that he let me down. I'm going to remove this burden by describing other ways that he can help. For example:

"Oh, that makes sense, I understand completely. Would it be okay if I used you for a reference instead? New clients often ask me who I'm working with and I prefer to give them names of people and organizations that they will recognize and respect."

OR

"Oh, that makes sense, I understand completely. How about this instead—the marketing company that develops my material is constantly after me to provide client testimonials. I prefer to give them the names of people and organizations that are recognized as industry leaders and respected for their

leadership. If they were to call you, would you be willing to offer a testimonial or an endorsement?"

I have never had a client say "no" to this request. They usually smile, feel flattered, and are more than willing to help. Everybody wins.

What if Bob's answer to my original referral request is, in fact, the one that I feared the most? What if Bob says:

"Scott, I cannot recommend you to anybody."

Okay, now it is time to run away. Just kidding. This is actually the best answer that I can get. Something has obviously gone terribly wrong with our relationship—certainly it is not what I thought it was or I never would have asked for a referral in the first place. Bob is not pleased—of that we can be sure. In fact he is so displeased that I was about to lose him as a client and I wasn't even aware that the relationship was in jeopardy. I can respond to this turn of events with much wailing and gnashing of teeth. Or, I can see it for what it really is—a gift. I have been granted the gift of a second chance; an opportunity to discover what is broken, to fix it, and to replenish the value, integrity, and trust that has dissolved. I may not be successful, Bob may be too far gone, but if I'm going to lose him, I'm going to lose him while trying to keep him.

Why am I willing to invest so much time and energy into a relationship that may have been soured forever? For a number of reasons:

> Chances are very good that the wound is fresh, otherwise I'd already be aware of it. If I work quickly and earnestly, it probably isn't fatal. If the wound is not fresh, however, news of it is, and I can presume that it was not painful enough for Bob to mention previously or perhaps he is just a silent sufferer, not prone to complain but needing to be heard. In either case, I've opened a door and I'm going to encourage Bob to walk through it. I want to hear everything that is troubling him, get it all out on the table, remain non-defensive, and convince him that I'm going to try and repair the damage.

> Customer service statistics have shown that your most loyal clients and your best source for references are those that have experienced a breakdown in service and you have worked on their behalf to try and fix the problem. Those that have never had a service problem with their account will usually tell 1–2 people about your good service while those that have had a service issue that you at least tried to correct will recommend you to 5–6 people. "Problems" are

really opportunities waiting to evolve. After I discover what Bob's problem is, I'm going to provide him with a detailed action plan that will specify exactly what I am going to do and when I'm going to do it. I will also forecast the probable outcome and double check that it matches his expectations. I will keep him updated every step of the way and, when I'm done, I'm coming back to Bob for a referral.

Remember, time is money. I will spend up to 20 times more money, time, and effort trying to replace Bob's account with a new client than I will if I try to keep him. Plus, I have worked very hard to get and to keep Bob's account. Obviously I did not fully understand every expectation that Bob may have had and there is certainly cause for concern—but not for surrender.

I have a reputation to protect. I know that I will never be able to fulfill every client expectation, all of the time. However, I should be aware of every client's expectation all of the time. If one got by me, I'll own it and do what I can to repair the damage. If they continue to get by me, the damage will be permanent. The statistics tell us that dissatisfied clients will tell 10–12 others about the poor service that they received. My world is too small to have that kind of message on the street.

The point is: always attempt to correct the problem. An ounce of prevention is definitely worth a pound of cure ... but a pound of cure is still worth the time.

We have demonstrated that a referral request is clearly not a simple "yes" or "no" proposition for either you or for your client. If we approach the question intellectually rather than emotionally, structure our request in a clear and deliberate format, relax our expectations, and simply listen to the response, something good will develop. On the other hand, if we stumble into it, stumble through it, and stumble out of it, we will never be quite sure of what the result will be.

After the Answer ... Giving Thanks and Following Up

Okay, you have asked for a referral, received a response, and it is time to move on to the next step. Starting with the most probable response, let's assume that your referral request harvested two referrals, one that hits pay dirt and one that leads to an undesirable account.

If you're like me, you will be tempted to immediately start chasing the qualified opportunity and you'll want to ignore the other. Considering the value of your time, this behavior would seem perfectly compatible with your need to be highly selective when allocating your time and when choosing which opportunities to pursue. Under normal circumstances, when you are the only one making the decision, this would be appropriate. In this scenario, however, the decision about which opportunity to pursue has been made for you. Your client, colleague, or center-of-influence has decided that both opportunities are worthy of your time and, out of respect for the referral provider, you are obligated to connect with both.

Let's remember what is at stake here. The referral provider has put his name on your marquee. He or she is framing the value, integrity, and trust that you have delivered along with their own story and allowing you to use it elsewhere. Yes, they feel great about giving referrals, but they do not give them casually or without concern for the outcomes. Rest assured that the next time the referral provider speaks with the person to whom you were referred, your name will come up. Imagine how embarrassed your friend will be if the other party has never heard of you.

Professional and consistent follow-up with both the referral provider and the new contact will guarantee a steady stream of new opportunities. Random and haphazard follow-up will close the door on them forever. So (no surprise), we need a proactive system to manage the referral harvesting process. Now for Step 6, A professional thank you and a commitment to follow up.

Acknowledging the fact that you received a referral, any referral, or that you are being considered for one is the first thing you must do. A hand written note or a formal letter is best for this purpose. You may also e-mail a card if you wish, but make sure that the referral provider is a "fan" of electronic mail. Here are four sample "thank you" letters that address the contingencies that we covered with "Bob". These are for you to use as a template for your own notes or letters.

Referral Thank You Letter:

Dear Referral Provider:

I would like to take this opportunity to express my appreciation for the referral to John Warren of Clayton Widget Manufacturing.

I am honored that you're comfortable enough with my agency and the level of service that I provide to recommend us to others. There is no better feeling than the one that comes from having a satisfied client who refers you to their trusted friends and business associates.

In the next few days, I will be sending John a letter of introduction and following up with a phone call. I'll be sure to keep you informed as things develop. In the interim, please feel free to call me if you have any questions or if there is anything I can do for you. Once again, thank you very much.

Sincerely,

Thank You For Considering A Referral Letter:

Dear Referral Provider

I would like to take this opportunity to thank you for considering me for a referral. I am honored that you're comfortable enough with my agency and the level of service that I provide to recommend us to others. There is no better feeling than the one that comes from having a satisfied client who refers you to their trusted friends and business associates

I will call you next week to discuss any contacts that you think I should make and to review a list of potential clients that I would like to meet. In the interim, please feel free to call me if you have any questions or if there is anything I can do for you. Once again, thank you very much.

Sincerely,

Thank You for Being A Reference/Testimonial Letter:

Dear Client:

I would like to take this opportunity to express my appreciation for allowing me to use your name as a personal reference and as a testimonial for the work that we have done for your organization.

I am honored that you're comfortable enough with my agency and the level of service that I provide to recommend us to others. There is no better feeling than the one that comes from having a satisfied client who is willing to endorse our performance both publicly and privately.

When the opportunity to use your name as a reference arises, I will be in the habit of calling to brief you on the prospect and the opportunity. I'll also keep you in the loop as things develop. In the interim, please feel free to call me if you have any questions or if there is anything I can do for you. Once again, thank you very much.

Sincerely,

Thank You for Being Honest Letter:

Dear Client:

Words cannot express how sorry I am that your account was not being serviced in a fashion that met with your expectations. Nor can they appropriately describe the embarrassment that I feel for being surprised by the news that we have disappointed you.

Needless to say, I am going to do whatever is within my power to do, so that I may regain your trust and reestablish our value as your Broker of Record. Enclosed you will please find a preliminary action plan that outlines the steps I will take to remedy the service gaps that you described.

Make no mistake about it, this work is my highest priority and it will remain so until you are once again satisfied. I will plan to follow up with you on a weekly basis, by telephone and through e-mail, to keep you updated and informed of our progress. Thank you for giving us a second chance. I assure you that we will not need a third.

Sincerely,

Notice that each letter contains a brief description of the next continuation step on your agenda. This is done to consistently keep the referral provider aware of what is being done and informed as to what to expect in the future. You do not want the referral provider to develop "referral remorse" or to feel left behind. These letters, or ones like them, should be written and sent as soon as possible. Certainly not later than the day after the conversation takes place and preferably the day of the conversation. Having done this, it is now time to approach the new contact(s) if you received a referral. If you did not receive a referral, comply with the continuation plan that you described in your letter. Be absolutely certain to proactively calendar all of your follow-up activities as described in Chapter Four – Priority Management. There is no margin for error.

Making the Introduction

Hallelujah! Like General Patton rolling through a liberated Paris on a Sherman tank, you're flush with victory and excited about the new opportunity. In fact, you're hardly out of the building before you reach for your cell phone to make the call to set things in motion. Then … you get voice-mailed or stonewalled by a gatekeeper. You dutifully leave a message, wait a few days for a response, try again, leave another message, wait some more, and … nothing. Your "referral missile" is looking more and more like a dud and you're feeling less and less positive about the efficacy of the whole exercise. Your calls seem like cold calls and the lack of response reminds you of the old days. Talk about disappointment.

What happened? Although you perceived your call to be credible enough to be accepted, it registered as just another cold call with the contact and was treated accordingly. Simply dropping the name of the referral provider was not enough to get you through the door because your call had all of the elements found in a traditional cold call. It was unexpected, you were most likely excited, and it appeared intrusive. Just another slick producer peddling product.

As you might expect, we suggest a more polished approach. First, take a deep breath and get a grip. There is no need to rush into the contact. Haste makes waste and all that. When you apply urgency you bring unwanted pressure on a potential opportunity that will not tolerate it. Give yourself, the referral provider, and the new contact time to develop a level of comfort and understanding (there's nurturing that garden again). The referral is as good next week or, for that matter, next month and next year, as it is today. Now, with sound mind and body, we move on.

In Channel Marketing we reviewed using a pre-approach letter to introduce who you are and why you are making the contact. Our method for presenting yourself to a referral contact is quite similar with the added benefit of notifying the referral provider that contact has been initiated. For example, you send the following introductory letter to the referral contact:

Sample Referral Approach Letter:

```
Dear Contact:

Your name recently came up in a conversation I was having with
MaryAnne DiCanto of Nice Premium, Inc. She suggested that you
and I make contact to review the risk management program that
we have custom-developed for Nice Premium and to explore the
potential for doing the same for you.

With MaryAnne's permission, I have enclosed some information
about our company and the program. I will call you next week
to formally introduce myself and to review this packet with
you in greater detail. In the interim, please feel free to
call me directly at (Phone Number), with any questions or
comments. Additional information is also available on our
website: www.youragency.com.

Sincerely,


CC: MaryAnne DiCanto
```

What do you think might happen when either MaryAnne or the referral contact receives their letters? Usually, one will contact the other and discuss who you are and what you are about. In the normal course of that conversation, MaryAnne will explain the reasons for her recommendation, review her program, and firmly establish your credibility and value. But wait, it gets better. She will then call you to summarize her conversation and provide you with greater insight and vital information. *Now* when you make your introductory call, you can expect that your call will be returned.

As an additional enhancement to this growing sense of camaraderie between the referral provider, the new contact, and myself, I will often suggest that the first meeting with the new contact take place over breakfast or lunch and include the referral provider. This technique makes the intro-duction much more comfortable and relaxed for everybody, affords me the opportunity to keep the referral provider active in the process, and actually allows me to witness somebody else selling me. Not only is it flattering, it is incredibly effective.

Wait, there's more. I cannot count the number of times that, during the walk or ride back from lunch, the referral provider starts enthusiastically discussing the next introduction that he or she is going to make for me. This is producer heaven.

Of course, on the heels of these meetings, everybody gets a thank you note. In fact every contact made during this process requires that a follow-up letter, note, card, phone call, or e-mail is sent to all parties. No exceptions. Here is another sample of referral approach letter—this one specifically designed for a channel market (the YMCA). **Please review all of the other sample letters located in** our Online Library. at: www.gopolestar.com. There are certainly enough ideas there to get you started. Next, let's review what to do when your referral turns into a sale.

Referral Approach Letter: Channel Market

```
Mr. Stephen Wayne
Your Town YMCA
2500 Main Street
Your Town, PA 18901
```

Dear Stephen:

Liz Louise of the Any Town YMCA provided your name to us. Liz suggested that we contact you to review the risk management audit process that we have just completed at the Any Town YMCA, and to discuss the feasibility of conducting a similar program for the Your Town YMCA.

Our extensive experience with nonprofit organizations, combined with this unique risk management assessment tool, provided Liz with an unbiased, comprehensive analysis of the facilities, staff, culture, and insurance program currently in place at the Any Town YMCA. Our final report contained a concise explanation of our findings along with a series of recommendations to enhance each location's risk management and loss control program. Working with select insurance providers, including the National YMCA Mutual Program, we were able to custom-develop a comprehensive strategy that is tailored to address the specific needs of the Any Town YMCA.

Attached you will please find a brief description of our agency and our process. Our record proves that this value-driven approach leads to enhanced program design, reduced premiums, and satisfied clients.

In the near future, I will call you to formally introduce myself and to review our program in greater detail. In the interim, please feel free to call me directly at————————
—with any questions or comments.

Sincerely,

CC: Liz Louise, Any Town YMCA

After a Sale

You are triumphant. Having patiently worked your referral harvesting system and enlisting the help of your trusted client, you have successfully developed another trusted client. You have created the ultimate Win-Win-Win. Everybody involved is feeling validated. You know what to do next with your new relationship—stay close, stay proactive, and stay involved. You know how important it is to remain visible and viable, especially so during the first few months following the transaction. What about the referral provider? Now that the circle has closed, what happens next in that arena?

Certainly you need to express your gratitude; however, sending yet another letter of thanks would be, at best, redundant. What can you do to adequately demonstrate your gratitude? Well, a gift would be nice; but not just any gift will do. You wish to give something special, something tangible, and something permanent. Something appropriate that will remind the referral provider of this wonderful episode in your relationship and also reinforce the goodwill that you have established. Here is our list of "Do's & Don'ts" for referral gift giving:

> **Do** give something personal; **don't** give a tacky trinket from the company store. Although your office closets may be overflowing with logo golf shirts, logo pens, and logo coffee mugs, this is not a marketing event. Save that stuff for the new accounts. Your gift should be selected based upon your personal relationship, not your professional one. If you know their taste in music, give a CD. If you

know their taste in clothing, give a tie or a scarf. If you see plants in their office, give an interesting plant, etc.

Do give something nice; don't give something lavish. There are laws in most States that place a specific dollar value limitation on non-taxable gifts. Additionally, many companies do not allow their employees to accept gifts from vendors. Tactfully find out what is appropriate for your referral provider. In the event that he or she is not permitted to accept a gift, a small donation to their favorite charity or something similar is usually acceptable.

Do give something permanent; don't ever give a "bottle". The booze-giving days of yesteryear are behind us forever and for good reason. Besides, there could be a nightmare, or a car wreck, an embarrassment, or a lawsuit in that bottle; don't take a chance. Instead, give a non-consumable gift that will serve as a permanent reminder of the experience. Flowers are nice ... but they die. Food is nice ... but it gets eaten up. Tickets are nice ... but the show ends. These gifts will be forgotten and we never want to be forgotten in any way. For example, the CD that was mentioned earlier—every time the CD is played, who is the referral provider going to think of? Every time the necktie or scarf is straightened in the mirror, who are they going to think of? Every time the plant is watered ... Every time the frame is viewed ... Every time the hat is worn ... You get the point. Are these positive or negative thoughts? Assuming that your taste is appropriate—they are both positive and permanent.

My personal favorite referral gift is a magazine subscription. Each month, the magazine arrives on my client's desk and it might as well have my picture on the cover. I get "Runner's World" for the runners, "Flying" for the pilots, "American Heritage" for the history buffs, and "The Coconut Telegraph" for the Parrot Heads. I make sure that all gift subscriptions are non-industry related.

A last thought on referral gift giving—most people enjoy being surprised by a gift and, when they are, they usually call to say thank you. When they do call, they often have some other ideas to work on and some additional people to see. And so it goes.

Next let's cover our final scenario. What do you do when nothing happens, when you are rejected or you do the rejecting?

When a Sale Doesn't Happen

Sometimes, despite your best effort to help the referral provider qualify the lead, you will get recommended to a misfit account—an account that doesn't meet the criteria established by your client profile.

Perhaps the account is too small, perhaps it is in the wrong industry, or perhaps it is an out-and-out deadbeat account. On other occasions, you will be recommended to an account that you may wish to write; however, they do not wish to be written by you. Perhaps they are happy with the incumbent, perhaps they are "lowest bid" buyers, or maybe you just didn't get along. Regardless of the reason for the rejection, we have some "bad news" to deliver back to the referral provider.

Earlier in this section, I briefly mentioned that we are obligated to follow through on all referral leads, regardless of our desire or ability to actually write the account or develop a relationship with the referral contact. We are bound by our integrity and the strength of our relationship to respect all recommendations and to protect the position of the referral provider.

Although this mandate does in fact contradict the precedent that we established in Channel Marketing and Priority Management, the follow-up strategy that we suggest is not terribly involved or time consuming. We need only to close the loop on every referral in a manner that is consistent with our overall value-added service strategy.

For the accounts that you deem inappropriate, send your referral approach letter anyway and follow-up with a phone call. Your discussion with the referral contact should be entirely focused on who they are and what insurance needs they might have. Once their needs are established, you will be able to determine if they are best served by staying with their current agent and insurance program or if you should refer them to another agency that could improve their service or program. Whatever the solution is, you maintain the role of insurance advisor rather than insurance agent. Once they are referred away to another agency or producer within your network, they usually stay away and you have still fulfilled your obligation.

In this instance, your follow-up call to the referral provider is very simple:

"Bob, I spoke with Jack Reynolds over at BigHazard, Inc. and we had a wonderful conversation. What an interesting guy. We reviewed the program that he currently has in place. We agreed that the insurance product was the right one; however, the company needs immediate loss control help. I gave Jack the names of two loss control consultants who I have worked with before and

would be of great value. Jack is going to connect with them and let you or me know what his impressions are. I've already called each of them and briefed them on the company."

OR

"Bob, I spoke with Jack Reynolds over at BigHazard, Inc. and we had a wonderful conversation. What an interesting guy. Based upon this preliminary review, I told him that I thought he was being under-serviced. I've given him the name of an agent friend of mine who specializes in Jack's industry and can really pull together a great program. I don't have access to the kind of program that Jack will need going forward. Even if the product can't be moved due to the firming market, my colleague will be able to help with proactive risk management and loss control. Jack is going to connect with him and let you or I know what his impressions are. I've already called the agent and briefed him on the company."

Regardless of the circumstances that you uncover, your opinion and advice is all that is necessary.

Your follow-up conversation regarding an account that you did pursue but didn't get is very similar:

"Bob, I met with Hilarie Williams over at A1 Riding Stables. We had a great meeting and, in the end, she determined that she is more comfortable staying with her current agent. We did agree to connect from time to time to discuss any new developments and she indicated that she would enjoy attending our next safety symposium. Thank you so much for the introduction, I absolutely love to meet new people and I was able to learn quite a lot about her industry. It was definitely time well spent."

Notice that in all of these conversations, we never let the referral provider feel as if they have failed. We must find something good to say about each contact that we make and let the referral provider see how the referral was beneficial for everyone. Finally, please remember to send everybody involved a thank you note and make sure that your colleagues follow-up with every referral that you sent his or her way.

Summary of the 10-step referral harvesting strategy:

Step 1 – Make a list of at least 20 potential referral sources, including:

- Existing Clients
- Centers-of-Influence
- Industry Service Providers
- Colleagues and Affinity Groups

Step 2 – Set a weekly referral request objective (minimum of 1 per week).

Step 3 – Decide when and how to make each referral request, either face-to-face or over the phone. Never through the mail!

Step 4 – Prepare a script for your request that:

- Discloses your intention
- Includes a "relationship reminder"
- Includes a professional request
- Includes a qualifying statement
- Reassures and assists
- Includes a professional thank you and a follow-up plan

Step 5 – Ask and respond appropriately

- If the answer is "yes", move to step 6
- If the answer is "I can't think of anyone", help them think and consider providing a list of desirable prospects.
- If the answer is "I don't give referrals", find out why, accept the reason, and ask for a reference or testimonial.
- If the answer is "I can't recommend you", find out why and commit to saving the relationship.

Step 6 – Immediately send a "thank you" letter that includes a description of your continuation plan.

Step 7 – Send a referral approach letter to every referral contact and copy the referral provider.

Step 8 – Follow-up each letter with a phone call to:

- Set an appointment with qualified accounts.
- Review, advise, and refer unqualified accounts.

Step 9 – Continue to update the referral provider on the status of each referral, including the "bad news".

Step 10 – Send a personalized thank you gift to referral providers that generate new business.

Please grant yourself an enormous advantage and learn to use this referral harvesting strategy. You cannot be successful or ever realize your true potential unless you have a fully developed system for harvesting and processing referral opportunities. Because your future depends on it, you cannot afford to be bashful, intimidated, lethargic, or unprofessional about building and working your personalized referral harvesting system. Those characteristics will only hold you back with countless others, so lose them quickly.

Remember that asking for referrals is truly an act of service, not an act of exploitation. You have worked so hard to earn this privilege but you will continue to work too hard if you do not take the time to harvest such opportunities. Over time, it can and will become your only method for generating new business opportunities, if you follow these guidelines and manage your system deliberately and consistently. You have come this far—now it is time to assume your rightful and hard-earned position at the top. Your referral harvesting system will provide you with everything that you need to get there and to stay there.

Chapter Ten

Final Thoughts

With years of instructing and coaching this process in my wake, I am elated to make it available to you without the need to fund or attend our in-person programs. That being said, I begrudge the fact that we are going to miss the opportunity to spend time together, one-on-one, to discuss your unique set of circumstances and your personalized adaptation of the material.

I can, however, predict what you will need the most help with and offer you the same advice that I would normally give to you in person.

Experience has shown that the most significant obstacle encountered by the participants of our in-person programs is "friendly fire" from within their own company. In most cases this is due to an instinctive, pre-conditioned response to change. Although nothing that you have designed could be categorized as "radical", much of what you will be doing certainly flies in the face of conventional wisdom and legacy behavior. Indeed, chances are good that you will upset the organizational apple cart.

While I can't be with you to help you help them see the light, I can offer you some suggestions that will reduce or eliminate the disruptions that can come from those who don't support your plans. Although most eventually do come around and see the merits of your approach, it doesn't happen overnight. It can be a bit discouraging. The following section will help you understand what is happening and offer you some tips to get through it.

Terrorized by Change - The Dilemma of Internal Innovation

The greatest single deterrent to organizational growth is the refusal by an organization's members to accept the change that facilitates the growth. We speak endlessly of new plateaus, new horizons, new business, and a new breed, yet most prefer to follow the familiar routine. We build magnificent plans, copy models, develop logos, create teams, conduct countless meetings and ... never move forward. We shake things up only to watch in frustration as those around us settle back in. Sometimes the mere suggestion of a simple adjustment in strategy is enough to make you wish you hadn't. Is it all worth it? Absolutely yes. In a market that is characterized by chaos and is searching to find itself, improved efficiency and effective differentiation are prerequisites to survival. Is there anything you can do to resolve the conflict between internal innovation and preconditioned responses to change? Not likely. Human nature prefers an established comfort zone and a predictable world. You can, however, lighten your load a bit by understanding the resistance while you continue to hold your position. Listed below are the three greatest challenges faced by those who dare to be different along with some ideas on how to manage the negativity.

Stick to your guns, trust your instincts, and no … nothing is easy.

Challenge # 1 – Everyone's a Critic.

Defending status quo by attacking the unfamiliar is the world's oldest *preoccupation*. Change shatters the illusion of control, safety, predictability, and wisdom found in all comfort zones. Although we can longer execute our pioneers, people still line up to terminate a new idea. Be leery of the "it-will-never-work …" Eeyore-worshiping, rain-on-any-parade, Chicken Little-like crowd, and hang with the believers. For those that understand what you're doing and support you in that effort, no explanation or justification is necessary. For those that don't and won't understand, no explanation is possible.

Challenge # 2 – The Illusion of Perfection.

Do it right, the first time, every time, right? Not. Especially not when you are creating, researching, and developing. Trial and Error are Life's greatest teachers and they demand flexibility, perspective, patience, and tolerance from their students. Perfection is a state of mind. You cannot and will not design and implement a new strategy that answers every contingency and fulfills every expectation. Your innovation will develop over time, not overnight. You are initiating and managing a process of change, an evolution, not an event. You must manage your expectations accordingly. Things in life rarely follow your plan with exactness, and people never do. Expect perfection and you'll always be disappointed. Loosen up; life is far too short to sweat every moment.

Challenge # 3 – Measuring Success.

Defining success as anything other than a tangible goal achieved or a positive result attained might seem absurd to the casual observer; however, traditional measurements of day-to-day success are not appropriate for innovative works in progress. Our greatest achievements, discoveries, and adaptations usually result from things gone slightly awry rather than according to plan. Our success is our participation in the process and our greatest measurement of that success is how well we participate. Simply doing the best that you can do, with what you have, moment-to-moment, day-to-day, and week-to-week until it is time to do something else is a fabulous achievement. Oh, this can be so much fun, or it can be misery; the choice is yours. Choose fun.

Finally, we have established a "Hard Market Selling" book club in our Polestar Community Center. This is a forum for our readers that you can access to get support, suggestions, and ideas from your peers as well as from me. To get there, please go to the Polestar website at www.gopolestar.com and left click on the "Community Center" link. In order to post, you will need to register. Simply left click on the "Register Your Free Account" link in the menu bar and follow the instructions.

Good luck and good selling.

Appendix

Sample Letters and Useful Forms

I have produced a series of forms and sample letters for your use in putting this book into practice. They are available in both Microsoft® Word® format so that you can modify them and in Adobe® Acrobat® format for your perusal, printing, or re-copying if you don't have Word. The online library contains a growing collection of templates, letters, marketing plans, and sample assessments that our readers and training program participants contribute on a regular basis.

We encourage you to use these tools and to submit your own as well so that we may keep our online shelves stocked and current. Please send your submisions to onlinelibrarian@gopolestar.com

Download them from www.gopolestar.com/downloads.

Shelf A contains:
  Sample Pre-approach Letters, Follow-up Letters, and other correspondence
Shelf B contains:
  Client Roundtable Development Kit
Shelf C contains:
  Client Seminar/Workshop Development Kit
Shelf D contains:
  Sample Needs Assessments and Action Plans

*This book was lovingly set in Adobe Minion types
by Michael Höhne.*